A DEEP BUT DAZZLING DARKNESS

Timothy Kinahan

A Deep but Dazzling Darkness

A CHRISTIAN THEOLOGY
IN AN INTER-FAITH PERSPECTIVE

the columba press

First published in 2005 by
the columba press
55A Spruce Avenue, Stillorgan Industrial Park,
Blackrock, Co Dublin

Cover by Bill Bolger
Origination by The Columba Press
Printed in Ireland by Colourbooks Ltd, Dublin

ISBN 1 85607 500 1

Table of Contents

CHAPTER 1

What is truth ?

But we make his love too narrow
By false limits of our own,
And we magnify his strictness
With a zeal he would not own.[1]

It is rigidity that divides us, not truth, for truth would set us free.[2]

He had already learned by experience that faith and doubt belong to-
gether, that they govern each other like inhaling and exhaling.[3]

Truth gains more by the errors of one who, with due study and prepar-
ation, thinks for himself, than by the true opinions of those who only
hold them because they do not suffer themselves to think.[4]

There is in God, some say, a deep but dazzling darkness.[5] So
Henry Vaughan, in the mid 17th century, struggled poetically to
come up with an image that could illuminate the Divine, especially as he/she relates to humankind.

Everyone struggles with words, because words are central to
communication, and communication to being human. But
words are notoriously fickle, taking on different nuances of
meaning as they move between different media, people, places
and cultures. A description of a landscape may have one person
in raptures, and leave another totally bored. To knock someone
up has a totally different meaning in America than in the UK.
Words that might once have comforted me now seem banal and
shallow.

Furthermore, it is highly unlikely that any reader of this book

1. From F. W. Faber's hymn *There's a wideness in God's mercy*, Number 9
in *Church Hymnal*, OUP, 2000
2. John V.Taylor, *The Go-between God*, SCM, 1972, page 24
3. Herman Hesse, *The Glass Bead Game*, Penguin, 1984, page 127
4. J. S. Mill, *On Liberty*, Everyman, page 94
5. Henry Vaughan (1621-1695), *The Night*, Stanza 9

will understand what I write in exactly the way I would like it to be understood. Each reader will react, almost chemically, to what I write in their own unique way, coming to it as they do through their varied filters of experience, nurture, attitude, preconception and subjective taste. Nobody ever hears exactly what we intend them to. That is inevitable, and enormously creative – but at the same time, it can be mighty frustrating !

But the problem of words – their joint role as obscurers and illuminators – causes immense problems for faith, which is dealing with many of the deepest things of human experience and Divine reality. Gandhi's comment that 'the very attempt to clothe thought in word or action limits it. No man in this world can express a thought in word or action fully'[6] gets close to the heart of the difficulty: if there are problems of communication on a humdrum domestic level, where we all at least think that we know what we are talking about, how much more magnified must those problems become when we seek to explain the Ethereal Other that is at the heart of faith?

Truth beyond words
That is one of the reasons why religious people have traditionally moved beyond words, using music, art, sculpture and silence to communicate their deepest desire. It is also one of the reasons that people have come to recognise that God communicates through these and other media. He does not limit himself to words. At the heart of the Christian revelation is the recognition that *Word* is central, but not enough. The *Word* becomes flesh,[7] becomes tangible, human, emotional, relational. The Word becomes a person. This has implications.

Jesus is recorded, in St John's gospel, as saying 'Whoever has seen me has seen the Father.'[8] Yet this same Jesus pointed out, in

---

6. Mahatma Gandhi, from a prayer speech 26 May 1946, quoted in Margaret Chatterjee, *Gandhi's Religious Thought*, Macmillan, 1983, page 110
7. John 1:14
8. John 14:9

his famous parable of the last judgement, that those who did good deeds to the poor and the oppressed were not just helping 'these brothers of mine', but Jesus himself.[9] This, along with Paul's repeated insistence that Christ dwells within his people, and his people in him,[10] suggests again that theology cannot just be concerned with making statements about 'God' but needs, rather, to be talking about humanity, and especially the marginalised of this world. Theology *is* anthropology, it is about people. It is about the *person-hood* of God.

Now, we all know about people. They are even more slippery than words. The one and the same person can be a brother, a father, an uncle, a son and a grandfather – sometimes all at once. The one and the same person can be loved, admired, detested and feared; regarded as a sage or as a loony; seen as kind and dismissed as manipulative and callous. No two people see another person in exactly the same way, either physically or personally. We come to the other person from different places, with different experiences, baggages and expectations, and inevitably therefore see them through different eyes. That is part of the rich web of human being, both enriching and maddening at one and the same time.

That the Word became flesh begs many questions, but the one that concerns me at this juncture is this why did God choose to clothe mis-apprehendable Word in slippery Flesh? Surely at least part of the answer must lie in his own nature, which we as human beings are supposed to reflect.[11] Incarnation – not mere analogy – shows that truth is more fully revealed in the personal than in the verbal or the propositional. Incarnation reveals that God wants – not just 'is prepared' – to be seen from many different perspectives and in many different ways. The category 'Word' was inadequate, too prosaic. Incarnation, person-hood, was needed more adequately to reveal the nature of the living,

9. Matthew 25:31-45
10. e.g. Romans 12:5; 2 Corinthians 5:17; Romans 8:10; Galatians 2:20; Ephesians 3:17 etc
11. Genesis 1:28

communicating God, with all the dangers that that entailed. Somehow God decided that it wasn't enough for humanity to get all steamed up about words. They needed something really confusing – a person who defied all previous, and all logical, categories. But the God of risks took the risk. Humanity needed to be freed from the limitations of confining word. 'Truth is not,' as Mother Maria of Normanby has written, 'a system of thought. Truth is not created. Truth *is*. Christ is the Truth. Truth is a *person*. Truth is not limited within our comprehension of it. Truth transcends us: we can never come to the full comprehension of truth.'[12]

Doctrine and Truth

I believe that this has profound implications for Christian doctrine. More precisely, I think that this has profound implications for the importance we attach to all our cherished theological and doctrinal formulations.

Theology and doctrine are important for Christians, and it is right that this should be so. We naturally desire to put into words the faith that is within us, and which we have inherited. Theology, as St Anselm put it,[13] is *faith seeking understanding*; doctrine gives structure to, and at least attempts to define the meaning of our faith: it puts that faith into a historical and communal, as well as spiritual and intellectual context. It helps us 'belong' to a particular church community, and hence to the body of Christ. But, because we are forced by our very humanness to use words as we undertake this task, we are doomed to be using the very medium that God himself outgrew by incarnation. The doctrinal formulations of our own particular tradition can help us on our path, as they contextualise the journey of faith, both historically, communally and theologically. But those doctrinal formulations are not themselves the faith, they are

12. Quoted in Kallistos Ware, *The Orthodox Way*, St Vladimir's Seminary Press, 1998, page 85
113. Anselm, *Proslogion*, Chapter 1. In *Anselm of Canterbury*, Vol 1,eds Hopkins and Richardson, SCM, 1974, page 93

only an attempt to understand it. They are a peep-hole onto reality, a one-dimensional black-and-white print-out of reality.

All credal formulations of doctrine are historically conditioned. They were never created in a vacuum, but in a specific historical context, in response to particular needs. In that specific context, doctrine was formulated as a 'best-fit', the best way to define belief for that specific world. But the world moves on, and as historical and cultural variables change, so too must the formulation of doctrine, insofar as doctrine is related to human and Christian experience. Tertullian, an early North African Christian, recognised this as early as the third century when he protested against what he saw as the overweening hellenisation of Christian theology in his day. Christian statements need to take account of who we are, where we are, and where we come from; they need to be related to the experience of the generation in question. Better words may be found to articulate the Christian truth for a new generation. All statements of doctrine must be provisional. Otherwise they risk fossilisation.

Truth as process
Does this mean that all theology, all attempts at 'faith seeking understanding' are doomed to failure? I think not, for the *process* of seeking understanding is vitally important: it gives to those who search a sense of quest and of relationship with God. I am attracted by Edward Conze's characterisation of Buddhist doctrine as a 'rallying point for meditation'.[14] Established doctrine, as stated in the previous paragraph, has an important part to play in the day-to-day experience of being in a faith-community: 'this is the way we do things, and think about things, when we seek to do the things of God and be the people of God.' While this remains true, and should remain true, it should also be clear by now that it is in the nature of words to be imprecise and of sentences (and the meaning those sentences seek to convey) to be provisional. Words, even words of great meaning, can only ever be a pale shadow of the ineffable, or what Hans Küng has

---

14. Edward Conze, *Buddhist Scriptures*, Penguin, 1969, page 181

called 'a conceptual approximation to the indescribable'.[15] They can only point to the truth, more or less accurately. They can never be the truth itself. As Anthony de Mello once pointed out,[16] when the wise man points to the moon, the fool sees only the finger. And the problem with doctrine is that it is all too often seen not as the finger that points, but as the ineffable truth itself.

This process, of mistaking doctrine for truth, words for reality, is something that we all do a great deal of the time. It is part of the human condition. Much of the time it doesn't matter, because we are all at least subliminally aware that we indulging in a mutually convenient shorthand that successfully lubricates the process of inter-personal communication. But for religious people the dangers are very real. Because we start to mistake our verbal formulations of truth for Truth itself, we set up barriers between ourselves and other folk on the religious pilgrimage whose circumstances, history and experiences have led them to different formulations. Perceptions of truth become a battleground, and Truth itself gets obscured in the resultant dustcloud. That is bad enough: but far worse, in many respects, is the fact that God himself is belittled in the process. Words have become deified, in stark opposition to the historical reality of the divine Word-who-became-flesh in order the better to communicate with us. We re-verbalise the incarnate Word. Doctrine turns into dogma, and dogma, of its very nature, become dogmatic and unyielding. God is belittled, hide-bound by inelegant covers of outdated verbosity. By insisting that it is only our orthodoxy that is orthodox and adequate, we are in fact saying that God is so small that he can only travel along one path at a time. We are saying that God is so limited that he can only reveal himself in one way. And to belittle God in any way is what our forebears would have condemned as blasphemy.

The Jews were aware of this: the more they searched for God,

---

15. Hans Küng, *Tracing the Way: spiritual dimensions of the world's religions*, (trans John Bowden), Continuum, 2002, page 53
16. in a video

the closer they became to him, the less confident they were about using his name at all. There seems to be an ambiguity at the heart of God, a quicksilver humour that always pops up in a different place with a laugh, as if to say 'aha, you thought you'd got me taped!' There is, of course, ambiguity everywhere: reality would not be reality without it – and in God, *ex hypothesi*, that ambiguity is hugely magnified. The nature of reality, as Alex Wright has said, 'depends on where and how you look at it. For example, birds are able to determine colours that are invisible to human beings … in these conditions, can it make any sense to say that only one perspective is 'true', and that there is no room for different layers of ambiguity?'[17]

It is sad that, so often, honest attempts to explore and explain faith have become set in stone; that the liberation of reformation itself becomes a prison because of our fixation with words. Words, although not usually literally set in stone, do tend to take on the nature of propositions; tentative explanations and theories become, over the years, to be regarded as sacrosanct. Words have an unerring tendency to encapsulate the truth in pill-sized chunks, to make cold proposition out of living reality; they limit the scope for journey, since once we have accepted the relevant proposition, we are already deemed to have arrived. Words as propositions (doctrine) leave little room for creativity, since propositional truth has a tendency to become absolute and in-variable. Truth-as-proposition leaves no room for inclusivity, since you either have the truth or you don't, are either for or against, either right or wrong. Issues of doctrine get used to ex-clude others, in the most unwelcoming of manners, in stark con-trast to the gracious welcome that we have received from God. Truth viewed in a propositional manner is a stark thing, cold and unbending, which ignores what Krishnamurti noted back in 1929, that 'truth cannot be organised.'[18] It is a poor vehicle with which to communicate the immense richness of Divine glory. It imprisons the human psyche in false and simplistic certainties.

17. Alex Wright, *Why bother with theology?* DLT, 2002, page 61
18. Jiddu Krishnamurti, talk on 2 August 1929. In *Indian Religions*, ed. P. Heehs, Hurst and Co, 2002, page 518

Karl Rahner notes the relative, provisional nature of theological inquiry, that 'every answer is only the beginning of a new
question'.[19] That attitude may be true for some of those engaged
professionally in theological inquiry, but it is all too rare
amongst the guardians of faith-tradition. The thinker who does
question tradition is all too often vilified, condemned as a
heretic, put in front of a consistory court or an inquisition, ex-
communicated – as has happened in most Christian denominations throughout history, even into our present century.
Christian denominations, often founded as the result of a doctrinal split, seem to equate their very integrity with the mainten-
ance of that original position, even when the historical context,
and the questions that go with it, have markedly changed.

Truth in certainty and ignorance

Of course, this doesn't have to be the case, but it all too often is.
We like certainty, especially in our oh-so-fluid world. We like to
feel that we can control things – and part of the illusion of language is that it imagines that it controls that which it names, just
as Adam named the creatures in Eden as a symbol of his mas-
tery over them.[20] But God cannot be controlled, except insofar as
he allowed himself to be dominated on the cross. Maybe the
cross is an affirmation that God is, in his self-emptying, willing
to be controlled by his creatures, but somehow I doubt it. Rather,
I see in his self-emptying and subsequent resurrection an affirmation that all attempts to control God are doomed to failure. The
God-who-was-so-much-bigger-than-mere-word had also to
show that he was beyond personality, beyond gender, beyond
form. Yet we continue to crucify him with our restrictive doctrines.

It is sad that so often in the history of man's religious quest,
especially amongst the 'people of the Book', words have in practice come to be the be-all and end-all of faith. When doctrine,
rather than the experience of the living God whom we worship

---

19. *Foundations of the Christian Faith*, DLT, 1978, 32
20. Genesis 2:19-20

in Spirit and in Truth, becomes over-important it becomes cold, confrontational and calculating. It needs the leaven of love, of an orthopraxy (right living) that shows its' orthodoxy (right belief) through open and transparent living.[21] Doctrine is an attempt to explain (as is all theology). It is a perception of divine truth that tends towards the Truth, as Aquinas put it.[22] It is important only insofar as it sheds light on God, or on the economy of our salvation. To vary De Mello's image – doctrine should be a torch illuminating truth. We would be wise not to idolise the torch. Indeed, the torch image could perhaps be developed in parallel with Jesus' suggestion that we should be the light of the world, 'incarnations' of living word who also point to the Divine Word – and similarly never to be mistaken for God.

We are in strange realms. Strange because we are not dealing with conventional certainties. We are not trying to describe the workings of a computer or the rules of chess – we are floundering on the edge of the infinite. Yet we do not flounder, because at the heart of faith is a belly-deep knowledge, something that is gut-wrenchingly and overwhelmingly true, a sure foundation whose very surety cannot be demonstrated either in words or mathematical equations. We are face to face with the God who 'dazzles us with an excess of truth'.[23] Every time I feel that I have said something profound or adequate about God, I have to remind myself that what I have said is only the merest approximation of reality, a whiff of the incense of heaven, an obscuring veil that must never be taken too seriously, let alone cast in stone. Simone Weil has articulated this well: 'There is a god. There is no god. Where is the problem? I am quite sure that there is a god in the sense that I am sure my love is no illusion. I am quite sure there is no god in the sense that I am sure that there is nothing which resembles what I can conceive when I say that word.'[24] Like Anselm, she is aware that God is 'that than

21. James 2:12-27; 1 Corinthians 13:1-3
22. *ST*, ii-ii q.1.9.6.
23. As the angel, in a paraphrase of Aquinas, said to St Francis in Olivier Messiaen's opera *Saint Francis of Assisi*
24. Simone Weil, *Waiting for God*, Harper and Row, 1973, 32.

which nothing greater can be thought',[25] and therefore in a fundamental sense inconceivable. Like Jalaudin Rumi, a Sufi poet of the thirteenth century CE, she would have agreed that 'The man of God is beyond faith and disbelief.'[26] It is the best words that are often the most dangerous, because they are the most likely to get taken too seriously.

Socrates, in recognising that his wisdom lay in the fact that he recognised his ignorance, was moving close to religious truth. Evagrius of Pontus (246-299 AD) regarded as blessed those who had 'reached the ignorance that is inexhaustible'.[27] Paul expressed it differently in his First Letter to the Christians in Corinth when he remarked that 'what seems to be God's foolishness is wiser than human wisdom, and what seems to be God's weakness is stronger than human strength'.[28] This would suggest to me that those of us who use words must do so with care, and not be beguiled by their undoubted power. We should recognise that even the best that we can say seriously underestimates the God who is the source of our creativity. Anything we say, if taken at face value, limits and circumscribes the infinite. The closer we get to God, the more we are forced into the recognition that all our profundities have hardly rippled the surface of the Marianas Trench of the Divine. We are forced to recognise that it is impossible for us to comprehend God in all his fullness and that 'the most we can ever hope to achieve is a partial revelation of God.'[29] We are confronted with the same reality as Job, who came to recognise that he had 'talked about things I did not understand, and marvels too great for me to know ... in the past I knew only what others had told me, but now I have seen you

25. Anselm, *Proslogion*, chapter 3. In *Anselm of Canterbury*, Vol. 1, eds. Hopkins and Richardson, SCM, 1974, page 94
26. In Idries Shah, *The Way of the Sufi*, Penguin, 1968, page 116
27. Evagrius of Pontus, *Gnostic Chapters iii.88*. Quoted in A. Louth, *The Origins of the Christian Mystical Tradition*, OUP, 1983, page 108.
28. 1 Corinthians 1:25
29. Teja Singh, *Asa di Var da bhav prakasani tika* (Amritsar, 1952) pp 24-28, in W. H. McLeod, *Textual sources for the study of Sikhism*, Manchester University Press, 1984, par 141.

with my own eyes. So I am ashamed of all that I have said, and repent in dust and ashes.'[30]

The necessity of searching

Having said that, it is still incumbent on the inquiring mind to try and explore faith and the things of God. Anthony de Mello makes the point with his customary simplicity:

The disciples were full of questions about God.

Said the master, 'God is the Unknown and the Unknowable. Every statement about him, every answer to your questions, is a distortion of the truth.'

The disciples were bewildered. 'Then why do you speak about him at all?'

'Why does the bird sing?' said the master.[31]

The questing spirit is to be commended – indeed, is vital to growth. I suspect that was, at least in part, what Jesus was referring to when he recommended that we become like little children,[32] for it is in the asking of questions, in exploration, that children mature and grow. The Christian scriptures encourage us to explore and ask questions like children,[33] but also to move beyond childish things[34] to more mature fare.[35] So we cannot shirk the responsibility of asking and seeking to answer the very questions we know ourselves to be ill-equipped to deal with. What I want to do is to put that responsibility in context.

There are writers for whom any attempt at theology is dangerous and misguided. Representative here would be Carl Jung: 'Every statement about the transcendental ought to be avoided, because it is a laughable presumption on the part of the human mind, unconscious of its limitations.'[36] The early Greek Fathers

---

30. Job 42:3-6
31. Anthony de Mello, *The Song of the Bird*, Doubleday, 1984, page 3
32. Mathew 18:3
33. ibid
34. 1 Corinthians 13:11
35. 1 Corinthians 3:2; Hebrews 5:12-14
36. quoted in F. C. Happold, *Mysticism*, Penguin, 1973, page 64

suggested that, 'if you think that you have understood something, then it was certainly not God'[37] – a thought that was taken up with enthusiasm by St Augustine of Hippo, amongst others. Johannes Eckhart, a German writer of the late thirteenth and early fourteenth century, spoke in similar vein: 'why dost thou prate of God ? Whatever thou sayest of him is untrue.'[38] On one level these writers, and those like them, are right: it is a laughable presumption for us to seek to describe the infinite in mere words. But at the same time there is a real human need for such statements and descriptions. Without them we would not be able to conceptualise God in any meaningful way, despite all the pitfalls and limitations. Theology becomes laughable, becomes false, when it is unconscious of its limitations, when it presumes to know in detail what in reality it is only pointing to. When theological enquiry becomes dogma, it is starting to take itself more seriously than God. All religious thinkers would do well to remember that, after he had had an overwhelming vision of God, all Ezekiel could do was to describe 'the appearance of the likeness of the Glory of the Lord'.[39] Even after such a close encounter, he could not describe God, or even the glory of God. Nor could he describe the likeness of the glory, but only the appearance of the likeness of the glory. If a prophet of God showed such temerity, what right have we to presume that our words are any more adequate or direct ?

There are others within the Christian tradition who have recognised the inadequacy of their efforts. St Augustine of Hippo (354-430 AD) noted that 'there is in the mind no knowledge of God, except the knowledge that does not know him',[40] yet went on from that fundamental premise to build up the theological foundations of Western Christianity. There would have been a part of St Augustine (but only a part, as his behaviour to-

37. quoted in Hans Urs von Balthasar, *Elucidations*, trans Riches, SPCK, 1975, page 18
38. quoted in Happold, op. cit., page 64
39. Ezekiel 1:28 (RSV)
40. quoted in Happold, op. cit., page 64

wards the Donatist schismatics makes horrifyingly clear) that would have been appalled at the way his thinking became the benchmark for orthodoxy. He would probably have approved of Sartres' comment that 'faith, even when profound, is never complete.'[41]

The best theology, like the best science, puts itself forward as a thesis – tentative, hopefully enlightening, but open to revision in the light of fresh evidence and new experience. It is an essay in exploration. Any theology that rests content with restating the same formulæ in what is basically the same language for each new generation is going to seem increasingly quaint and irrelevant, an old-tyme religion that has not kept up with the times. For theology to speak at all it needs to resonate with the life we now live, taking into account the realities of modern day life and experience, the discoveries of science and the advances in technology. There is always the possibility that we will, at some stage, be forced to say 'Yes, I was wrong. My picture of God was inadequate. I need to revise it.' Faith has to contain within itself the acknowledgement that it might be illusory. Otherwise it is mere knowledge.

This process can be seen taking place in the pages of scripture itself. The very earliest pictures of God in the Bible are of a tribal God – the God of Abraham, of Isaac, of Jacob and Israel. When David left Israelite territory he felt that he could no longer worship the God of Israel, but only the 'foreign Gods' of the Philistine people in whose territory he was now living;[42] and the Book Judges seems to suggest that, while the Lord is the God of Israel, so too Chemosh is equally validly the God of Ammon.[43] This was the 'local' God whom Naaman the Syrian wanted to worship, so he took with him a load of Israelite soil so that he could do so even in his far-away home.[44]

As the years went by, and Israel's experience of the world grew, the prophets of Israel began to note that this picture of

41. Jean Paul Sartres, *Words*, Penguin, 1969
42. 1 Samuel 26:19
43. Judges 11:23 ff
44. 2 Kings 5:17

God was seriously wanting. The prophets of the eighth century BC and after lived in a situation in which the political dreams of both Israel and Judah lay in ruins, when her leading citizens were either dead or in exile. This led many to abandon the traditional worship of their ancestors, and follow the obviously more powerful gods of Babylon, such as Marduk. Faced with this mass apostasy the prophets, of whom 2nd Isaiah is the most powerful example, began to drive home the less than obvious message that the God of Israel was the only God, besides whom the other so-called and seemingly powerful gods were 'useless'.[45] 'Besides me there is no other God; there never was and there never will be.'[46] That was, of course, implicit in Israel's faith from Day One, but it took time for the Spirit to lead his people to an acknowledgement of that particular truth.

Similarly, the earliest pictures of God in the Old Testament are of a powerful, almost mountain-god figure, whose presence is accompanied by fire and earthquake,[47] a very sighting of whom can lead to instant death,[48] a somewhat capricious,[49] vindictive[50] and ruthless figure. These pictures were never entirely abandoned,[51] but they were considerably mellowed by the people's experience, and by their belief that this same God also demanded of them the highest standards of honest and integrity, especially in their dealings with the less fortunate members of society. There is a progression in understanding from those rather blood-thirsty passages to

> Yet I was the one who taught Israel to walk,
> I took my people up in my arms ...
> I drew them with cords of affection and love,
> I picked them up and held them to my cheek;
> I bent down to them and fed them.[52]

45. Isaiah 41:29; 44:9
46. Isaiah 43:10
47. Exodus 19
48. Genesis 16:13; Judges 13:22
49. Leviticus 10:1-3
50. Exodus 32:25-29
51. Hebrews 12:29
52. Hosea 11:3-4

In the early days of Israel's existence, wandering around the wilderness as a nomad people in the days before the conquest of Palestine, they almost literally saw themselves as carrying their God around in a box – the Ark of the Covenant.[53] But this too was soon seen as an inadequate idea, and it was not long before the people were being reminded that this God did not dwell in a house made with human hands,[54] but was the cosmic Lord of all creation.[55]

Examples could be multiplied, and some scholars might choose to question my chronology in places, but the point is none the less made: there are different pictures of God within the pages of the Bible. Not all these pictures are compatible. They make for a rich tapestry, a creative tension, in which the biblical authors struggle with the limited words and concepts available to them to project a believable and coherent picture of God. Many of the later writers must have felt that they were dwarfs standing on the shoulders of giants: but even as dwarfs, they saw further, and further enriched both themselves and us. The biblical writers were part of a process, being led into all truth,[56] not as legalists enforcing the incontrovertible letter of a moral or theological law.[57]

Much of scripture, of any tradition or faith, uses poetry – either directly (as in the Psalms or the Song of Solomon) or by allusion (as so often in the prophetic literature). Poetry cannot be taken literally: it is full of simile and metaphor, which only have meaning if not taken as literal, prosaic truth. Poetry is often a vehicle of truth because it uses words as an anvil, hammering out alternative meaning and looking beyond the written word. But that can only happen if it is not taken literally. Poetry points to truth, it is not truth itself.

The essence of what I am trying to illustrate at this point is that we can say very little that is definitive about God. If scrip-

---

53. 1 Samuel 4:6
54. Isaiah 66:1-2
55. Isaiah 40:21-31
56. John 16:13
57. 2 Corinthians 3:6

ture itself can be tentative and developing in places, we ought not to be too afraid to rethink, or at last rephrase, our most cherished credal formulæ.

A Truth for belonging

There is a real dilemma here. On the one hand we need words to explain what we believe, while on the other hand words are constraining, limiting, and confusing. Words help us to understand what we believe, but at the same time they can actually obscure what they are seeking to explain in a fog of seeming adequacy. We need doctrine, we need creeds, both on the human and intellectual level. But how do we deal with these doctrines and creeds once we have them, so that they can be a positive and creative influence, rather than a dead weight that kills?

I feel that this is a question of parameters – where do we, in the Christian community, draw the lines beyond which someone can be deemed to have excluded themselves? Should we draw such lines? I am not sure that there can be a definitive answer to this, as every group and individual will want to place the boundaries in different places. We will each have a point, a cherished belief, that we believe to be essential, a *sine qua non* of any coherent understanding of God. Yet the very fact that there are so many such points suggests that in the real world we will all have to settle for very fluid parameters, porous boundaries. We will have to recognise that there are many people of integrity who will see things differently, who may have seen things in God that we have failed to notice, or whose experience of life will have caused them to inter-react differently with the Divine, in much the same way as oxygen reacts in different ways with hydrogen or sulphur. 'There is no reason,' as St Teresa of Avila put it, 'that we should want everyone else to follow our own path'.[58]

God is incomprehensible, and part of incomprehensibility is its inability to be rationalised or tied down. Rationalise incomprehensibility, despite the very natural human tendency to do

---

58. St Theresa of Avila, *Moraduas*, 3.2.18.

so, and it disappears. It can be argued that doctrine, when applied correctly, is an attempt to protect the ineffability of God from undue rationalisation. Much in Christian experience that passes for dogma, such as the doctrine of the Trinity, is in fact little more than an attempt to formulate in words the contradictory consistency of the mystery of God, thus protecting him (and us) from more simplistic and less satisfactory formulations. As Hans Urs von Balthasar has said:

> The Christian centuries and millennia have repeatedly erected towering theological buildings around these mysteries. From time to time it becomes necessary to stress the insufficiency of much that has been thus heaped up in order to make room for new attempts. In the event it is no more than a start, an attempt, and approximation, just as the shared life between two lovers remains to the end a start, an attempt to find a way to each other, but only as each allows the other his own freedom. Woe to the lover who, by whatever means, were to seek to tear from his loved one the final secret! Not only is such an attempt impossible, but also by it he destroys the life of love.[59]

There is here almost a love-hate relationship with doctrine: necessary but dangerous; vital but potentially very destructive, both for ourselves in our relationship with God, and for God as he gets defined out of mystery.

Perhaps, for a community's self-understanding, there is a need for a clear cut-off point, one which says 'beyond here, you don't really fit in'. Questions of belonging, and of shared understanding, are important. But to go from that to the issuing God-like anathemas is presumptuous in the extreme. It seems to me that when religious groups delude themselves into thinking that theirs are the only 'true' formulations of the evidence, they are slipping into arrogant delusion, revealing their own insecurity by insisting that theirs is the only security. They are mistaking thesis for fact, and unilaterally taking upon themselves the role

---

59. Han Urs von Balthasar, op. cit., page 24

of guardian of the faith. They are the followers of Ezra, who wanted to excommunicate everyone who was not of pure Jewish blood and faith, rather than followers of Jonah (who had to be taught that even the hated Assyrians could respond to God)[60] or Isaiah.[61] They – we – are lacking in humility. There may, after all, be some truth in the old Hindu axiom:

> In any way that men see me, in that same way they find my love:
> For many are the paths of men, but they all in the end come to me.[62]

There is an understandable fear of being seen to abandon 'sound teaching'.[63] But 'sound teaching' does not have to be seen in terms of intellectual assent to credal formulæ. Sound teaching is much more, in the New Testament, a case of good living. Jesus, in St John's gospel, talks of *doing* what is true.[64] The writer of 1 Timothy refers to 'lawbreakers and criminals … the godless and the sinful … those who are not religious or spiritual … those who kill their fathers or mothers … murderers … the immoral … sexual perverts … kidnappers … those who lie or give false testimony or who do anything else contrary to sound doctrine.'[65] The implication is that sound doctrine ('truth') is a good moral life, not a set of dogmatic propositions. This is borne out later in the same book, where we are told that 'if anyone does not take care of his relatives, especially members of his own family, he has denied the faith and is worse than an unbeliever.'[66] Or, in Titus, 'They claim to know God, but their actions deny it.'[67] Indeed, in the whole of Titus, 'sound doctrine' is defined in terms of behaviour, not in terms of the acceptance of certain

---

60. Jonah 3:5
61. Isaiah 56:1-8
62. *Bhagavad Gita* 4:11
63. 2 Timothy 4:3
64. John 3:21
65. 1 Timothy 1:9-10
66. 1 Timothy 5:8
67. Titus 1:16

propositions about the faith. As Jesus put it, 'by their fruits shall you know them.'[68]

This scriptural emphasis on orthopraxy is well-echoed in the outside world. Raja Rammohan Roy, back in the nineteenth century, noted that he regretted 'that the followers of Jesus, in general, should have paid so much greater attention to enquiries after his nature than to the observance of his commandments.'[69] And more than one African Christian theologian has commented to the effect that the followers of traditional religion on that continent 'are hostile to words unrelated to actions, and to doctrines unrelated to the earth and life.'[70] And I would add that, in his Beatitudes,[71] Jesus blessed a wide range of people, but not those of doctrinal purity and expertise !

I have a suspicion that the churches' long-standing fixation with credal fomulae has as much to do with control as with truth. Concern for orthodoxy, in the academic sense, is very much a churchy thing: those in positions of ecclesiastical authority have traditionally been the best educated, and they have guarded the esoteric truths of gospel almost as thought they were gnostic knowledge, without which salvation could definitely not be assured. But now that churchmen are often less well educated or articulate than the laity, this credal control is being challenged, and challenged by folk who also know their scriptures, and who are perhaps even better capable of reading the signs of the times than the isolated ecclesiastics. In short, prophesy is moving away from the institutional church, and the institutional church is not sure how to cope.

In the formulation of belief, all Christian groups are dealing with basically the same evidence: that of scripture, and that of experience. The former is problematical in that is avowedly viewed in such a multiplicity of ways; the second is also prob-

68. Matthew 7:16
69. Raja Rammohan Roy, quoted in S. D. Collet, *The Life and letters of Raja Rammohan Roy*, London, 1900, page 141
70. André Karamaga, 'Dialogue, an Evangelical Adventure' in *The Ecumenical Review*, Vol 39, No 1, January 1987, page 57
71. Matthew chapter 5

lematical, in that each of us has a different set of experiences. But
there is a bottom line: all Christian groups regard the Bible as to
some degree normative and important. All Christian groups, no
matter how they divide on detail, see Jesus as central. And all
Christian groups have experienced, in some way or another, the
reality of the transforming power of God. All the rest is commentary.[72]

This is a huge area of common ground, and one that is all too
often lost sight of in the internecine wars that have plagued
Christendom since the early days. It is a common ground that
should lead to excitement when we notice how others have re-
acted differently to it, and grown up differently in relation to it.
The New Testament is full of variety, as its writers explored
their own, and their community's, relationship to the same Jesus
with something akin to incredulity in their excitement. They
were struggling to find words adequate to the explosive impact
of their experience of him. To suggest therefore that God will
randomly condemn those who do not believe in the same way as
we believe is to make him into a very unattractive tyrant, a God
in our own unpleasant image. It is a demonisation of God.

Another unfortunate result of this codification of doctrine is
that we can very easily shut ourselves off from God: we close
our eyes to him because he sneaks in along unexpected paths.
There seems to be the presumption in many circles that God cannot be found outside the church – narrowly defined as our own
particular denomination. This limits God by assuming that we
can tell him what paths to follow. The basic theological truth,
surely, is that it is God who comes to us, who reveals himself to
us, not the other way round.[73] We deprive ourselves by refusing
to countenance the possibility that he may move in ways more
mysterious than we imagined.

---

72. Rabbi Hillel (c BC40-AD20), b.Shab.31a. Quoted in W. D. Davies,
Paul and Rabbinic Judaism, SPCK 1970, page 64
73. 1 Timothy 1:9; Quran 1:7, 2:41

Personal Truth

Faith is something that I hold very dear. Somehow it lends purpose and meaning to my life, giving it depth and direction when all else around seems to be in a state of chassis.

Yet, this faith is a slippery animal, defying easy definition: indeed, I am tempted at times to say that it is this very incorporeality that makes it what it is. I am not sure that meaning is enhanced by definition, just as I am unconvinced by attempts to tie down the numinous. Yet, as an articulate human being, I need to articulate, and to some extend account for, the faith that is within me. It cannot be wordless, so long as I remain human.

Here is a conundrum: the details of what we believe are important in that we all need some sense of religious structure and place in order to make sense of our faith-world. On the other hand, the moment we get too pernickety about the exact words we use to define the content of our belief, we run the risk of stifling that very religious impulse that makes that faith important. In religion we are dealing with a vast complex of beliefs, emotions, stories, histories, communities – and that is even before we begin to get involved with theological minutiæ. None of these, on their own, are easily pinned down: imagine how much harder it is to come up with anything sensible when all these complexities are so inextricably entwined! Faith is dealing with a value-added dimension, the dimension of the spirit. Of its nature it can never be pinned down. Yet the urge to do just that is always there.

In St John's telling of the last supper story, Jesus tells his disciples that the Holy Spirit will 'lead them into all truth'.[74] In other words, Truth is not something which the disciples, at that stage, were in full possession of. Truth was the goal to which the Holy Spirit would gradually lead them. It is almost as though Jesus was promising them a slow drip revelation, a growth in awareness, a deepening of experience, not a once-for-all flash of illuminating light. He was promising a journey as well as a destination, a journey with God towards God. To me (who, despite

---

74. John 16:13

the latitude that I would like to afford to others, am fairly traditionally orthodox in many ways!) that means being led into that
perfect relationship which is at the heart of God – the Trinity. The
Trinity is diversity, who reveals within his/her own person the
perfect unity of integral diversity; the Trinity in whom the Three
are more unified than one; the Trinity who reveals to us, through
relationship, the way in which diversity is central to any
Christian concept of wholeness. The Holy Spirit leads us into that
relationship of persons of which he is the glue and the inspiration
– not into a proposition, a creed, or a doctrinal formula.

Nevertheless, I share with other Christians the need to say
something about he/she whom I have experienced. In the normal run of things I want to say something about the people I
meet in day-to-day life, and especially about the people I love. I
find it relatively easy to say things about the Prime Minister, because I do not know him in any depth. I find it harder to say anything meaningful or permanent about my wife and children, because I know them and love them so much more than words can
convey. I know at least hints of their hidden depths. How much
more in the case of God, whose hidden depths and mysterious
ways are mysterious and profound beyond any meaningful
measure.

John Wesley, the founder of Methodism, once wrote: 'We
must both act as each is fully persuaded in his own mind. Hold
fast to that which you believe is acceptable to God, and I will do
the same ... let all these smaller points stand aside. Let them
never come into sight. If thine heart is as my heart, if thou lovest
God and all mankind, I ask no more: give me thy hand.'[75]
Wesley, in this at least, was a man before his time, recognising
kindred spirits on a similar journey, travelling through their
own territory with and towards of the same God. He, at least,
recognised that vital commonality and, while still holding firmly
to truth-as-he-saw-it, was humble and open enough to leave the
judgement on these matters to God.

---

75. John Wesley, sermon on 'The Catholic Spirit', quoted by Kenneth
Greet in *The Tablet*, 27 August, 1983, page 821

CHAPTER 2

An Interfaith Perspective

I can clearly see the time coming when people belonging to different faiths will have the same regard for other faiths that they have for their own.[1]

Consort with the followers of all religions in a spirit of friendliness and fellowship.[2]

I don't have the right or possibility of resolving the question of other beliefs and their attitude to the deity.[3]

I come from Northern Ireland, which in religious terms at least is a very traditional society. Within my own Protestant community, conservative evangelicalism is the dominant force. In such an environment, many people are deeply suspicious of ecumenism, let alone interfaith dialogue.

At the same time, I find that within my own (Anglican) tradition at least, a very real questioning of many of the old dogmatic certainties. Much of this questioning takes place privately for fear of being seen as 'betraying the gospel'. Needless to say, I do not see either ecumenism or interfaith dialogue as betrayals of anything: rather, I see them as vital expressions of my faith, and an integral part of my response to both God and his world.

Fear of other faiths

Yet the fears are real, especially when faith is seen in propositional terms. And these fears are not limited either to Northern Ireland or to the Christian community. They are a natural, if un-

1. Mahatma Gandhi, writing in the *Harijan*, 2 February 1934, page 8
2. *Gleanings from the Writings of Bahá'u'lláh* (1817-1892). Wilmette, Illinois 1976, page 95
3. Leo Tolstoy, *Anna Karenina*, trans R. Pevear and L Volokhonsky, Allen Lane, 2000, page 816

necessary, concomitant of the way most of us have been brought up to think of our own faith traditions.

There is, firstly, the fear of syncretism, whereby people mix and match different bits of different faiths to their own taste and convenience. Syncretism is generally frowned upon because it is incohesive – which is to say that it does not stick together in a coherent whole in a way that the mainstream religions would recognise. It was this that so irritated the Old Testament prophets, and elicited some of their most spectacular denunciations. The Old Testament Israelites – at least those who were on the receiving end of the prophets' wrath – were syncretists in that they tended to worship both Baal and Yahweh, as though they were taking out a double insurance policy. But, as Stanley J. Samartha has pointed out, syncretism such as this 'leads to spiritual poverty, theological confusion and ethical impotence.'[4] Instead of getting the best of both worlds, the syncretist gets the best of neither, since he is taking neither seriously. That is at least part of the reason that the Old Testament prophets inveighed so trenchantly against them. As Elijah said to the people on Mount Carmel: 'How much longer will it take you to make up you minds? If the Lord is God, worship him, but if Baal is God, worship him.'[5]

Yet this fear is soon dispelled by genuine and respectful dialogue. Outside New Age circles, where such syncretism is the name of the game, I have never met so much as a hint of syncretism in any inter-faith gathering. Rather, there is a mutual listening, an emphasis on the distinctiveness of various traditions, and an openness to allow that very distinctiveness to be mutually illuminating.

Opposed to this, I would argue that there is such a thing as an honourable and constructive syncretism, one that recognises the ultimate inexpressibility of truth:

---

4. Stanley J.Samartha, 'The Holy Spirit and People of Other Faiths' in *The Ecumenical Review*, Vol 42, Nos 3-4, July-October 1990, page 252
5. 1 Kings 18:21

> She (truth) has confused all the learned of Islam
> Everyone who has studied the Psalms,
> Every Jewish Rabbi,
> Every Christian priest.[6]

This is a kind of blurring of traditions that seeks to cut through the obvious problems to what lies at the heart of faith:

> There is no difference between a temple and a mosque, nor between the prayers of Hindu or a Muslim. Though differences seem to mark and distinguish, all men are in reality the same. Gods and demons, celestial beings, men called Muslims and others called Hindus – such differences are trivial, inconsequential, the outward results of locality and dress ... Allah is the same as the God of the Hindus, Pruran and Quran are one and the same. All are the same, none is separate; a single form, a single creation.[7]

This is a mystical tradition that somehow sees itself as transcending faith boundaries, while at the same time remaining nurtured by and loyal to its own traditions:

> Now I am called the shepherd of the desert gazelle,
> Now a Christian monk,
> Now a Zoroastrian,
> The beloved is three, yet one,
> Just as the three are in reality One.[8]

There is a small Christian monastic community in the Syrian desert whose website[9] publishes an interesting article subtitled 'In Praise of Syncretism'. Yet, this article is not really in praise of syncretism as commonly understood, for it is scathing of 'an omnivorous syncretism bordering of the pseudo-mystical delirium of schizophrenia, kitsch syncretism, without noble roots or the

---

6. Ibn El-Arabi (1165-1240 CE), in Idries Shah, *The Way of the Sufi*, Penguin Books, 1974, page 86
7. Dasam Granth, in W. H. Mcleod, *Textual sources for the study of Sikhism*, Manchester University Press, 1984, page 57
8. Ibn El Arabi, op. cit., page 87
9. www.deirmarmusa.org

possibility of fertile prospects.'[10] It is, rather a plea for a lived inter-
faith experience, a 'joint spiritual path',[11] in which Christianity
can recognise 'the mystery of the living God already effective in
the religious world of Islam'.[12] Deir Marmusa seems to be a
place where the monks are content to plunder the spiritual riches
of other traditions, while remaining firmly rooted within
Christian orthodoxy. There is a difference between what we
commonly understand as syncretism, which is a lazy and eclectic thing, and what we see at places like Deir Marmusa, which is
a constructive and humble engagement with the mystery of the
other.

There is, secondly, the fear of relativism, which places all religions on an equal pedestal. This might be possible to a dispas-
sionate academic, but to those who enter dialogue from within a
faith tradition, it is all but impossible. Relativism suggests that
we surrender our critical faculties at the door of dialogue –
something that is verging on the impossible for those whose
own faith is confident and secure. Relativism and syncretism are
only realistic dangers if we enter into dialogue unconvinced of
the value and saving efficacy of our own faith tradition. If we are
comfortable in our own faith tradition we have nothing to fear
save new insights.

A third fear is that of apostasy, actually converting, as did the
Augustinian missionary priest Fr Auguste Dupuis who converted
to Islam in the early years of the twentieth century,[13] taking the
name Yakouba; and the former Roman Catholic Uniate-Caldean
bishop of Uramiah, David Keldani, who took the name 'Abdu 'l-
Ahad Dawud.[14] Such apostasy, or conversion (depending on
your point of view) is extremely rare, for the same reasons as
stated above, but it can happen. Yet I do not believe that that

10. Paolo Dall'Oglio, *Ambiguous Syncretism and syncretistic ambiguity: in
praise of syncretism*, published on the web, page 2
11. ibid, page 6
12. ibid, page 7
13. William Seabrook, *The White Monk of Timbuctoo*, Harrap, 1934
14. 'Abdu 'l-Ahad Dawud, *Muhammad in the Bible*, Islamic Propagation
Centre International, Durban, 1990, page 7

should deter us. A road that is totally safe is rarely very interesting or rewarding.

A fourth fear – or rather criticism – of the whole interfaith enterprise is the belief that any level of tolerance, sympathy or understanding is inevitably merely subjective. By assigning any value whatever to the belief and experience of other faiths, we are taking a step back from our own exclusive authorities and traditions, and are allowing personal factors and inclinations to cloud our judgement. Don't our various scriptures and councils anathematise those who follow other gods? Isn't our whole church structure based on the premise that we, as baptised and believing Christians are 'saved', while others are still on the road to perdition? If our faith is 'true' in any way at all, surely it must mean that other faiths are false – and if false, then worthy only of our scorn.

Opposition to other faiths

This last criticism – that the whole enterprise is irredeemably subjective – is central to any opposition. To those coming from a biblicist or fundamentalist background the case at first seems watertight. The scriptures of all the main Judaeo-Christian traditions contain passages that are pretty clear-cut in their condemnation of 'the opposition', or condemn their gods as worthless. Within the Judaeo-Christian tradition the worship of 'other gods' is high on the list of things that the people of Israel must not do. The first commandment, after all, is 'worship no God but me.'[15] At the dedication of the temple, Solomon's final prayer concludes with the words: 'and so all the nations of the world will know that the Lord alone is God – there is no other. May you, his people, always be faithful to the Lord your God.'[16] The Second Isaiah was decidedly rude about these 'other gods' and their worshippers: 'all who make idols are worthless, and the gods they prize so highly are useless. Those who worship these

---

15. Exodus 20:3 (GNB)
16. 1 Kings 8:60

gods are blind and ignorant, and they will be disgraced.'[17]
'Besides me there is no other god; there never was and never
will be.'[18]

The Quran is equally devastating: 'If anyone desires a religion
other than Islam, never let it be accepted of him; and in the here-
after, he will be in the ranks of those who have lost (all spiritual
good)'.[19] To Muslims Jesus is no more than a messenger of
Allah[20] and not in any sense divine,[21] who did not die on the
cross.[22] These are fundamental denials which, for many, make
dialogue a total waste of time.

The scriptures of Buddhism, Hinduism, Sikhism and
Bahá'íism are less inflexible, coming as they do from a very different place. Their traditions tend to be more accommodating
and eclectic, at least from the Judaeo-Christian standpoint – yet
in that they all fail to acknowledge the centrality of Jesus, many
Christians see dialogue as pointless, or at the very least a tacit
compromising of the uniqueness of Jesus Christ. The only appropriate approach, on this argument, is to proselytise.

Yet – and many have told me that this is a very subjective
'yet' – I find myself unable to deny that people of other faiths do
have a very real experience of God. I may not be able to articulate my faith and experience in the same language as they do; I
may even find some of what they say about God difficult to accept. But I cannot ignore what they have experienced, nor the
spark of God I see in their lives. This inability to deny their deepest experiences has two foundations: experiential and theological.

First, experiential. Having travelled in non-Christian coun-
tries, and lived amongst and dialogued with people of diverse
faiths, I have no doubt whatever that their experience of God is
every bit as valid as my own. I have felt the intensity and power

---

17. Isaiah 44:9
18. Isaiah 43:10
19. Quran 3:85
20. Quran 4:171; 5:75
21. Quran 5:17; 5:72
22. Quran 4:157

of their prayer, which has often put my own into the shade. This first struck me when travelling through the Sahel region of West Africa as a young man in the early 1970s: I travelled much of the time by public transport, small pick-up trucks with benches in the back called *taxis de brousse*. These would halt at the appropriate hours of prayer so that people could get off, place their prayer mats of the ground, and prostrate themselves it the direction of Mecca. Their prayer was a powerful stimulus to my own, so that I soon learned to join them by stepping aside and saying my own prayers in my own way. Their faith was stimulus to mine and struck me as every bit as life-enhancing as my own. Their awareness of the pervasive presence of God appeared every bit as rich as (if not richer than) mine. This experience is not unique to me – indeed others such as Henri le Saux (who took the name Abhishiktananda), and Dom Bede Griffiths have lived it at a remarkable and life-long depth, and communicated it with remarkable richness and integrity in their writings over the years.[23] To deny that reality seems to me to be wilfully arrogant and also – more significantly – to be saying that God is incapable of revealing himself except along ways that we recognise, or along paths that we accept as canonical. If God is omnipotent, surely he is bigger than that.

The Methodist writer, J. Neville Ward, has put this very well when talking about Jesus: 'In his oneness with God he certainly appears to millions of others in other forms, to which they give stories and names from the vocabulary of their own spiritual traditions.'[24]

God in other faiths

And that is the crux of my second, theological, objection to exclusivism. It is not just a subjective hunch, or mere wishful thinking, to believe that these folk have been touched by God. It is, rather, a theological certainty that, if God is God, he must be

---

23. Abhishiktananda, *Prayer*, SPCK, 1967; Bede Griffiths, *The Marriage of East and West*, Collins, 1982
24. J. Neville Ward, *Five for Sorrow, Ten for Joy*, Epworth Press, 1971, page 91

amply able to cross cultural and mythic barriers – indeed, to use those supposed barriers as pathways of his self-revelation. God is not in the business of barriers: he lives for self-communication. If God can speak through people and the wonders of creation – which he undoubtedly can – then he must also be big enough to speak through other faith traditions. '"Can these hundreds of millions of people be deprived of the highest good, without which life has no meaning?" He pondered, but at once corrected himself. "What am I asking?" he said to himself. "I'm asking about the relation to the Deity of all the various faiths of mankind. I'm asking about the general manifestation of God to the whole world ..."'[25]

People of other faiths have a real experience of God. They have a real experience of revelation. Why would God deny them that, just because they have not been able to hear the Christian gospel? As the Quaker apologist Robert Barclay put it as long ago as 1678, 'Isn't it a bit uncharitable to claim that, even though they could have been saved, none were?'[26] How could a loving God throw them to perdition just because their circumstances, or Christian incompetence, have made it impossible for them to find the Christian message attractive? As Stanley J. Samartha has put it : 'The question today is not so much *whether or not* the Spirit is at work among people of other faiths, as to *discern* the presence and work of the Spirit among those who live outside the boundary of the church ... Christians are called upon to *discern*, not to *control* the spirit.'[27]

Of course there are large differences, even direct contradictions – but the same can also be said within the boundaries of the larger Christian tradition. But even with these differences, the open-minded observer can learn a great deal from a different faith perspective. Islam's 99 beautiful names of God, for instance,

25. Tolstoy, op. cit., page 815
26. *Barclay's Apology in Modern English*, by Dean Freiday, Manasquan, New Jersey, 1967, Proposition 6, comment xxv, page 113
27. Stanley J.Samartha, 'The Holy Spirit and People of other Faiths', in *The Ecumenical Review*, Vol 42, Nos 3-4, July-Oct 1990, page 259

are an inspirational well of significance for anyone who would seek to know him better. Even a casual perusal of the Hindu *Bhagavadgita* or *Upanishads* can be most uplifting, even to the most jaded of minds. If my argument in chapter 1 holds any truth whatever, then the very provisionality of our own doctrinal formulations should alert us to aspects of value in the formulations, scriptures and experiences of others.

There has always been a (minority) view within the mainstream Christian tradition of scripture that is at least open to other experiences of God. Jewish, Christian and Muslim scripture are, obviously, full of denunciations of idolatry, and of the futility of following other paths: but to condemn idolatry does not necessarily mean that genuine spiritual experience is also denied. Within the Old Testament it was at times recognised that the God of Israel was also the one God of all mankind.[28] The covenant with Noah and his descendents was understood as a universal covenant with all mankind and all creation,[29] and not just with the chosen people of Israel. Israel, furthermore, was also to be a light to the gentiles, and not just the private possessor of an exclusive revelation.[30] The God of Israel was active in the history of all the surrounding nations, whether they knew it or not,[31] and could use even pagan kings as messiahs to fulfil his purposes.[32]

St Paul, in his famous address to the Areopagites in Athens,[33] takes as the basis of his proclamation the apparently self-evident truth that all people of all nations seek after God 'in the hope that they might feel after him and find him'. One possible interpretation of St Paul's remarkably eirenic and inclusive words is that Jesus is the fulfilment of all that is best in man's religious quest, an imprimatur of all human sincerity. He certainly neither

28. *A New Dictionary of Christian Theology*, ed Richardson and Bowker, SCM Press, 1983, page 95, upon which the next few lines are based.
29. Genesis 9:8
30. Genesis 12:3; Isaiah 49:6; 66
31. Isaiah 10:5
32. Isaiah 45:1
33. Acts 17

dismisses nor belittles the Athenian approach to God: rather, he builds on it as a worthwhile foundation for something larger.

Religious continuity

It is almost as though Paul was using the Athenian pre-Christian quest for God as an 'Old Testament' – a significant, although partial, revelation of God to a particular people at a particular time. He was not the last to do this: there has always been a strong tradition within Christianity of seeking a continuum between the religious past and the religious present, with the pre-Christian past an Old Testament fulfilled by the Christian revelation, which is seen as an answer to all the deepest unfulfilled longing of a people's particular past. The very concept 'Messiah' (or 'Christ'), although literally translated as 'anointed one', is a sufficiently absorbent concept to include within it all the deepest religious longings of any people, at any place, and at any time. The Messiah, if he is to be Messiah in any meaningful sense, must be the fulfilment of all people's deepest dreams, and not just of Jewish dreams. Otherwise Christianity would have never spread as far as it has. The opening words of the Epistle to the Hebrews need to be universal if they are to have any meaning: 'In the past God spoke to our ancestors many times and in many ways ... but in these last days he has spoken to us through his Son.'[34] It almost seems as thought the writer is saying that God speaks in different times and in different places – in different contexts and in different cultures – in ways that are most appropriate to that time, that place, that person, that context. And, because of the variety of individuals and contexts, it is hardly surprising that there is little superficial consistency. Consistency in matters as profound as this would, anyway, be rather like a monochrome rainbow.

This building on the pagan past as a *preparatio evangelica* can be instanced in many parts of the world. Dante Alighieri regarded Aeneas and Paul as in some way parallel figures, the former being 'regarded in such a worthy light' by God, and the latter as

---

34. Hebrews 1:1-2

'one who took the same trajectory' as his illustrious predeces-sor.[35] In early Christian Ireland many of the first churches were built on old pagan sites: on the one hand saying that the old had been supplanted by the new but also, subliminally, saying that this new fulfils the old, that there is no absolute dysfunction be-tween what has gone before and what is here now. Many of the early Christian saints of Ireland (and Europe), such as St Brigid, seem to have exhibited 'pagan' characteristics, or even have been pagan figures subsumed into the Christian myth. And pagan festivals, such as the Robigalia of 25 April and the feast of Natalis Solis Invicti on 25 December, could easily be 'baptised' into Christian meaning – such as, in this case, the Rogation tide processions[36] and Christmas day itself.[37]

In many parts of the world today there are more formal movements that seek to go back into their pre-Christian past in order to discover the ways of God. In New Zealand the Atuatanga movement seeks to delve into the Maori past and dis-cover the true voice of God struggling through the figure of Io-Matua-Kore.[38] Sometimes this can take the form of local people naturally looking over their shoulders in order to express the felt continuity between past and present. In the Solomon Islands people have tended to move from the interior to the coast when they become Christian. They have wanted to symbolise their new life in Christ by living in a new place by the sea. Back in 1963[39] a group of Anglicans had chosen what they thought was a good site. Some of the elders decided to consult a woman who had the power to call the spirits of the ancestors. The ancestors were called, and their arrival was heralded by a low whistling wind. They agreed to check this new land and report back a few days later.

35. Dante Alighieri, *The Inferno*, Canto II, 13-28, trans Ciaran Carson, Granta, 2002
36. Thomas O'Loughlin, *Celtic Theology*, Continuum, 2000, page 149
37. *Oxford Dictionary of the Christian Church*, OUP, 1974, page 280
38. *Anglican Taonga*, Easter 2002, pages 4-5
39. This story was related to me in January 1982 by an anthropologist at the Melanesian Institute course in Goroka, Papua New Guinea.

At the agreed time everyone gathered at the woman's house, and were informed that the site was acceptable, and that the ancestors were in favour of the move. One of the elders then asked the ancestor what he and his fellow spirits thought of this new religion, this 'lotu'. 'We see happening,' he was told, 'what we always longed for. We see a red glow where there was only darkness.'

In his letter to the Roman Christians, Paul suggests something similar, right alongside his insistence on justification by faith alone, namely that the 'Gentiles who do not have the law do by nature what the law requires', and will be judged on an equal basis as those who have known the law of Christ since their cradle days.[40]

Tolerance

The New Testament does speak of Jesus as the only way,[41] but that does not preclude the possibility of people coming to God through Jesus Christ without ever being able to name him. Jesus came to reconcile all things (and not just all people) to himself[42] so it is that reconciliation, in whatever context it occurs, rather than the personal credit, that must surely concern him. On this reading of these supposedly exclusivist texts, wherever we meet people who have had real, life changing experiences and revelation of God, that experience has been made possible by the work of Jesus Christ, the Word made flesh. Similarly, Jesus also defined his role as to reveal the Father,[43] not to glorify himself. So, wherever God is known, then there is the work of Jesus made manifest. God the Father is also found in religious systems other than our own – and there is Jesus, silently and modestly about his work of revelation. As Archbishop William Temple notes in his seminal commentary on St John's gospel, 'all that is noble in the non-Christian systems of thought, or conduct, or

---

40. Romans 2:12-16
41. John 14:6
42. Colossians 1:20
43. John 14: 8

worship is the work of Christ upon them and within them. By the Word of God – that is to say, by Jesus Christ – Isaiah and Plato, and Zoroaster and Buddha and Confucius conceived and uttered such truths as they declared. There is only one divine light, and every man in his measure is enlightened by it.'[44]

That is a very Christian way of looking at things, not always well received by members of other faith-communities. It is merely mentioned here as an example of how we can push out the boundaries of traditionally exclusive texts in order to under-line the mutual inter-penetration of all true faith. Again, we make God into someone very small if we dismiss that possibility outright. Christianity becomes as idolatrous as any other reli-gion when it begins to confuse itself (and its scriptures) with the infinitely subtle, pervasive and enigmatic reality of God. I have a great deal of sympathy with the inclusivist thought of Sri Ramakrishna: 'The dogmatist says: "My religion alone is true, and the religions of others are false." This is a bad attitude. God can be reached by different paths.'[45] There is, of course, a very real way that the dogmatist has logic on his side. But that is only the case if truth is taken to be synonymous with propositional truth. Religious truth goes deeper than that.

Within the traditions of other faiths there is a similar minority tradition of tolerance. In the Qur'an, where the 'people of the Book' refers to Jews and Christians, there are three texts that stand out:

– 'To you be your Way, and to me mine.'[46]
– 'Truth stands out from error: whoever rejects evil and be-lieves in Allah hath grasped the most trustworthy handhold, that never breaks. And Allah heareth and knoweth all things.'[47]
– 'of the People of the Book are a portion that stand for the

44. William Temple, *Readings in Saint John's Gospel*, London, Macmillan, 1974, page 9
45. *Rama Krishna, Prophet of a New India*, trans Nikhilananda in Victor Gollancz, *Man and God*, Houghton Mifflin, 1951, page 13
46. Quran 109:6
47. Quran 2:256

right ... they believe in Allah and the Last Day; they enjoin what is right and forbid what is wrong; and they hasten in emulation of all good works; they are in the ranks of the righteous. Of the good they do, nothing will be rejected of them; for Allah knoweth well those that do right.'[48]

The Hindu tradition, not surprisingly, is much more open to this kind of possibility. The *Bhagavadgita*, for instance, suggests that 'even those who in faith worship other gods, because of their love they worship me,'[49] and 'for many are the paths of men, but they all in the end come to me.'[50] This is typical of Hindu inclusiveness, even in more recent times: the twentieth century mystic, Anandamayi Ya noted of God that 'because he is infinite, there is an infinite variety of conceptions of him and an endless variety of paths to him.'[51] The Sikh faith is also more than open to other revealed truth, Guru Nanak himself remarking 'how many approaches to God and servants of God.'[52] The Baha'i faith preaches the essential unity of religions, and its founder Bahá'u'lláh remarked that the differences between the great religions are 'to be attributed to the varying requirements of the ages in which they were promulgated.'[53] And within much of traditional African religion 'evidence from our sources shows clearly that African peoples consider God to be both active and interested in the historical and ethical affairs of men'[54] – an area of common ground which has significantly hastened the advance of both Islam and Christianity within the African continent.

The Profligate God
All these are examples of our various scriptures struggling with

48. Quran 3:113-114, see also 3:115, 199 and 4:162
49. *Bhagavadgita* 9:23
50. *Bhagavadgita* 4:11
51. in Heehs, op. cit., page 545
52. A Selection of the Hymns of Guru Nanak 4.1.19.10, in Whitfield Foy, *Man's Religious Quest*, Croom Helm, 1978, page 274
53. *Gleanings from the writings of Bahá'u'lláh*, Bahá'í Publishing Trust, 1983, page 288.
54. John. S. Mbiti, *Concepts of God in Africa*, SPCK, 1975, page 244

the paradox of a temporally and culturally bound revelation and the eternal and trans-cultural immensity of God. There really are problems with claiming that our faith is the only way, for such claims almost inevitably imply that God is so small that he cannot come to people except along paths that we recognise and approve of. That, surely, is to belittle him – or even to put ourselves in the blasphemous position of seeking to dictate to God. Is he so miserly with his benefits that he distributes them only to those who have had the opportunity to hear about him in certain, culturally specific ways? Is our God so small that he can only come to people who wear certain labels? Religious exclusivism reveals the smallness and poverty of our own minds, rather than the inexhaustible riches of the limitless God. Exclusivity makes God into a very small, petty and insecure tyrant, devoid of love. I, for one, want nothing to do with such an unattractive God. And neither, I suspect, do most of those outside the churches who regard our jealous and petty positioning as rather pathetic.

There is a problem here. By and large our scriptures are exclusivist. Yet, the God those same scriptures portray is such that any such exclusivism seriously belittles him. Words, or at least our use of words, have trapped God in definitions and limitations that make him seriously small, have reduced him to absurdity. Yet the God of the Christian scriptures (at least) is a God of prodigal grace, lavishing hospitality on his undeserving children.[55] As any Calvinist will tell you, we are put right with God by God's grace, and not by our faith. Is it not therefore possible that this same God puts other folk from other faiths right with him as well? He is, after all, the God of surprising initiatives. For it is by grace that we are saved, and not by works.[56] We are saved by the utterly outrageous and profligate generousity of God. His grace is not grace if we think that we can limit or control it. We underestimate the power of God's forgiving

---

55. Luke 15:11-32
56. Ephesians 2:8

love if we think that we can limit it to within our own belief system.[57]

There seems to be a tendency at work here: the tendency to limit God (and our own vision) to places and opinions with which we are generally familiar. In our insecurity we tend to hold the unfamiliar at arms' length, because it threatens our supposed security and impinges radically on our comfort zone. Understandable though that might be, it is unhelpful from the scriptural, psychological and sociological point of view.

The Jew was enjoined to welcome the stranger and, indeed, finds in the act of welcoming the stranger that God is a great deal bigger than they had previously imagined.[58] This welcoming of the stranger, the quintessential outsider is, according to Marc Gopin, a litmus test of the ethical conduct of the majority group. The stranger is one who is both different but who is also 'to be included at Jewish celebrations, cared for and even loved.'[59] I would go further and suggest that the act of welcoming the outsider implies some degree of welcome and hospitality for his faith and his culture, regardless of whether we agree with it or not. If we make space for the stranger, as he is, we must also make space for his thoughts, his feelings, his faith, his experience, no matter how uncomfortable they may make us. For, after all, it is those things that make him what he is.

The Christian is likewise enjoined to the imitation of Christ, who broke down barriers between people and races.[60] The Christian is enjoined to move from hostility to hospitality, to embrace the unfamiliar. He is enjoined to love.[61] This does not mean that we uncritically swallow everything that the alien has to offer, but rather that we meet it on a level playing field. Here was can suspend judgementalism (for judgement is of God) and

57. Choan-Seng Song, 'The Power of God's Grace in the World of Religions' in *The Ecumenical Review*, Vol 39 No 1, Jan 1987, page 54
58. Ruth Patterson, *A Song for Ireland: journeying towards reconciliation*, Veritas, 2003, page 93
59. Marc Gopin, *Between Eden and Armageddon*, OUP, 2000, page 6
60. Ephesians 2:14-16
61. Matthew 22:37-40

come with open minds to see glimmers of God where perhaps we would previously have seen only darkness or a blur. God moves in mysterious ways, and we run a severe risk of not noticing him if we refuse to countenance the possibility that he might be generous enough to reveal at least some new truth about himself within faith systems that are strange to us. 'If we just stay in our own familiar zones,' as Kosuke Koyama has said, 'love comes weak from lack of exercise'[62] – and not just love, but also our understanding of the greatness and goodness and depth of the living God. We cannot in honesty dismiss someone else's experience of God, or his attempts to speak of God, since our own attempts can never even begin to do justice to the infinite God we both claim to worship and serve.

There is also, within all religious traditions, a strong tradition of creation-centred spirituality – one that looks at the created world and senses that 'the hand that made thee is divine':

'The heavens are telling the glory of God.'[63]

'Wise men in their meditation ... have seen the power of God concealed in his attributes. He is the one who directs all he causes.'[64]

'We believe that Allah has endowed us with the faculty of the intellect, and that he has ordered us to ponder over his creation, noting with care the signs of his power and his glory throughout the entire universe as well as within ourselves.'[65]

Just as people of all faiths (and none) can feel the redeeming touch of God when they encounter him in his creation (or in the inspired creation of artists and musicians), so too he is all around us[66] and within us.[67] God is Spirit,[68] and in both Hebrew

62. Kosuke Koyama, *Three Mile an Hour God*, SCM, 1979, page 75
63. Psalm 8:1
64. Shvetashvetara Upanishad 1:1-3
65. Muhammad Rida Al-Muzaffar, *The Faith of Shi'a Islam*, The Muhammadi Trust, 1982, page 1
66. Psalm 139:7-12; Acts 17:28
67. Ephesians 3:17
68. John 4:24

and Greek the words for spirit are also used for breath and wind, that life-giving though untouchable reality that is all around us, within which we live and move and have our being.[69] Once we become aware of that numinous presence we have come in touch with the living God, whether we can name that experience or not. Some people attempt to put names and definitions on that experience, in all its variety. That is a natural human tendency, basically good and valuable: but it ceases to be good and valuable when it takes upon itself pretensions of infallibility. The only infallible is truth itself, something that is bigger than any words or formulations can ever be.

God first, religion second

There is a story, popular amongst those who seek to compare and contrast the various faiths of the world, that concerns four blind men and an elephant. One of the men takes hold of the creature's tail, and affirms that an elephant is long and thin and hairy. Another feels the animal's side, and likens an elephant to a wall, warm and leathery. The third man feels that elephant's trunk and decides, with good reason, that elephant is like a snake. And the fourth man feels the animal's leg, and likens his discovery to finding a creature that is remarkably like a thick post set in the ground. None of these men were wrong, but they were each only partial in their appreciation of the elephant. So too, the application of the story goes, with our appreciation of God: each of us has some of the truth, but the nature of God is that he is bigger than any of our partial visions can ever be. That is his nature. As John Hick has put it: 'When a Muslim speaks of Allah the Qur'anic revealer, and a Hindu speaks of Brahman as the limitless transpersonal consciousness, they are not referring to two parts of reality but to two ways in which the limitless divine reality has been thought and experienced by different human mentalities forming and formed by different frameworks and devotional techniques.'[70] 'When light is experiment-

69. Acts 17:28 (where Paul is quoting Epimenides).
70. John Hick, 'The Theology of Religious Pluralism' in *Theology*, Sept 1983, Vol lxxxvi No 713, page 335

ed upon in certain ways it exhibits wave like properties, and when experimented upon in another way, particle like properties. We have to say that in itself, independently of interaction with human observers, it is such as to be capable of being experienced under different experimental conditions in these different ways.'[71]

Theocentric religion needs to orbit itself around God, and not around faith-systems or dogmas. But all too often we slip into the false position of defending our systems as the only way: belief in God becomes a belief in the system which, for all its merits, is as good at obscuring as revealing the divine. Religious people become locked in an internecine war that only belittles the whole concept of religion: we project an image that says to those outside that we are more interested in internal politics and internal perceptions of purity than we are in either people or God. Those outside the church, or faith-systems generally, are understandably hostile to words that bear little relation to actions, and to doctrines that seem unrelated in any meaningful way to the realities of daily life. Those outside look at the religions of the world and despair, even when they had come to us with open and sympathetic minds. In the words of Radhakrishnan, penned prophetically before World War II, 'If the great religions of the world continue to waste their energies in a fratricidal war, instead of looking at themselves as friendly partners in the supreme task of nourishing the spiritual life of mankind, the swift advance of secular humanism and moral materialism is assured.'[72]

Theocentric religion, as I have said, orbits around God – yet, for much of the time, we tend to orbit around our faith-systems, protecting those systems rather than seeking to promulgate the things of God. The founders of all three great faiths of the Judaeo-Christian matrix were very much Theocentric, seeking to put God first, and to sweep away much of the extra-religious

71. ibid, page 337
72. Sawepalli Radhakrishnan, *Eastern Religions and Western Thought*,)UP, 1939, page 247

contemporary baggage that was obscuring him. The first of the Jewish Ten Commandments reads: 'You shall have no other Gods before me.'[73] Jesus' primary revelation was of the Father;[74] and Muhammad was utterly relentless in his preaching of an undiluted monotheism. Coming at this, once again, from a Christian perspective, it would seem that Jesus revealed and mediated with a new intensity and insight what was always there in God. Forgiveness, salvation and redemption have always been central to the person of God, and can be amply illustrated from the scriptures of all three faiths. Neither Jesus nor Muhammad revealed anything new, but rather underlined and lived aspects of the Divine person that had become somewhat clouded. Jesus did not come to glorify himself,[75] but to give glory to the Father. Faiths other than Christianity also seek to give glory to God, each in its own unique way. They are not a conspiracy designed to obfuscate or confuse. They should be welcomed, with critically open arms, as fellow believers in a dangerously secular world, as fellow gropers after the inexplicable divine. To do otherwise is to move in an opposite direction from that which was travelled by Jesus himself.

Christians proclaim Christ Jesus as the way, the truth and the life.[76] That is our experience. But that does not mean, as the Roman Catholic Church has acknowledged, that we should reject anything 'of what is holy and true in these religions'.[77] Christians – and followers of other faiths – have for too long impoverished themselves by their blind dismissals of the followers of other faiths as mere infidels, idolaters or the great unsaved. There is too much richness, too much of God, in other faiths for us to remain content with judgemental ignorance.

In the famous prologue to his gospel, St John talks of the true

73. Exodus 20:3
74. John 14:8-11
75. John 8:54
76. John 14:6
77. Declaration on the Relation of the Church to Non-Christian Religions, Vatican II, *Nostra Aetate*, 28 October 1965, section 2

light that enlightens every man coming into the world.[78] He does not talk of the incarnate word merely enlightening a chosen few – but strongly suggests that everything in this world which is good and true and insightful, comes from God. By our inherited judgementalism we risk shutting ourselves off from the God we claim to follow and adore. Of course there are dangers attached, the dangers that we began with: of syncretism, relativism, subjectivism and apostasy. But they are small dangers when compared with the infinite riches that God is aching to share with us if only we would open our eyes ...

---

78. John 1:9

CHAPTER 3

The Experience of Liberation

Bourgeois salvation is congealed salvation.[1]

God and salvation are not exhausted by our particular experience.[2]

All that was left was total, luminous, clarity; perfect understanding; infinite freedom and unrestricted creativity.[3]

Salvation: the forgiveness of sins

A central tenet of the Christian faith, in virtually all its forms, is that salvation is given to us in the person of, and through the work of, Jesus of Nazareth. The New Testament is also fairly insistent that 'salvation is to be found through him alone.'[4] St Paul talks of Christians being set free by the sacrificial death of Christ – 'that is, our sins are forgiven',[5] and Peter, in his sermon to the Gentile Cornelius, says 'that everyone who believes in him will have his sins forgiven through the power of his name.'[6]

Christian writers, from the earliest times, have known this as a deep personal and corporate truth – indeed, as the fundamental truth of their Christian experience. This is perhaps best illustrated by a brief selection from Christian liturgies which, of their very repetitive nature, burn themselves indelibly into the consciousness of the faithful:

> O Lord our God, who showed your immense love towards us and sent your only Son into the world to rescue us from the ties of sin ...[7]

1. K.Kuitert, quoted in E. Schillebeeckx, *Christ: the Christian Experience in the modern world*, SCM, 1980, page 757
2. E. Schillebeeckx, op. cit., page 756
3. Kulalanda, *Principles of Buddhism*, Windhorse Publications, 2003 page 15
4. Acts 4:12
5. Ephesians 1:7
6. Acts 10:43
7. from the Ethiopian Orthadox Liturgy. Peter Day, *Eastern Christian Liturgies*, Irish University Press, 1972, page 134

Blessed are you Father …
For in your love and mercy
You freed us from the slavery of sin,
Giving Your only begotten Son to become man,
And suffer death on the cross to redeem us;
He made there the one complete and all sufficient sacrifice
For the sins of the whole world.[8]

Or, from the realms of poetry, which similarly etches itself onto the human psyche:

The time is ripe and I repent
Every trespass, O my Lord.
Pardon me my every crime,
Christ, as Thou art merciful.

By Thy incarnation sweet,
By Thy birth, my sacred King,
By Thy lasting baptism here
Pardon me my every wrong.

By Thy hanging, filled with love,
By Thy rising from the dead,
All my passions pardon me,
Lord who art truly merciful.[9]

Or hymnody, which is perhaps the most influential of all religious forms, certainly within Protestant Christianity:

Rock of Ages, cleft for me,
Let me hide myself in Thee.
Let the water and the blood
From Thy riven side which flowed,
Be of sin the double cure
Cleanse me from its guilt and power.

---

8. Eucharistic Prayer from *The Book of Common Prayer* of the Church of Ireland, Columba Press, 2004, page 210
9. Translated from the tenth century Irish of Oengus Céile Dé by Thomas Kinsella, *New Oxford Book of Irish Verse*, OUP, 1986, No 45

Not the labours of my hands
Can fulfil Thy law's demands;
Could my zeal no respite know,
Could my tears for ever flow,
all for sin could not atone;
Thou must save, and Thou alone.

And today Christians still talk of 'being saved', of the wonders of the atonement, of reconciliation with God, of peace with God … These, and many other phrases are used in various attempts to put words to the basic experience of liberation, of being free from an oppressive weight, of being given a free and direct access to the Father.

Salvation through Christ alone ?
To most Christians throughout the ages it has been a received article of faith that this salvation, being uniquely available through Christ, is therefore only available to those who specifically call upon his name. It is therefore a salvation only available to Christians, and anyone outside the church is condemned to hell. Various branches of the church have, over the centuries, attempted to narrow this down even further by suggesting that there is no salvation outside the fellowship of their own particular denomination: Pope Boniface VIII declared that 'there is one Holy Catholic and Apostolic Church, outside which there is neither salvation or forgiveness of sins',[11] a view that has been reaffirmed repeatedly.[12] This seems to leave little room for manoeuvre when asking whether salvation is offered to – let alone granted to – people of other faiths.

To many Christians, this proposition is self-evident: why else did Christ die ? If salvation were available elsewhere, then surely his death was a superfluous waste of time. I do not believe this to be the case.

---

10. Hymn by Augustus M Toplady (1740-78). No 557 in *Church Hymnal*.
11. *Unam Sanctam*, 1302
12. e.g. *Singulari Qundam*, 1854: 'it must, of course, be held as a matter of faith that outside the Apostolic Roman Church no one can be saved.'

It seems to me that the whole concept of salvation is but one model to help us to understand the work of Christ. Salvation, 'being saved', atonement, peace with God, eternal life, are all concepts employed by the New Testament and later Christian writers in their attempts to explain the explosive impact of Jesus. Yet they are all to some extent inadequate. The traditional view that Jesus saves (which of course has its origin in scripture) carries with it the suggestion that, although true, before Jesus God was somehow different. Before Jesus God did not save and was judgemental, unforgiving. A God who demands the substitutionary atonement of his only son in order to unleash his forgiveness is a coldly legalistic God and very much at odds with the loving Father who is so much at the heart of Jesus' preached message. It is also difficult to square the traditional view of substitutionary atonement with the very real message and experience of forgiveness and divine acceptance that occurs repeatedly in the Old Testament, not least within the Prophetic corpus and in the Psalms. My suspicion is that, in his death as in his life, Jesus was showing us what God the Father is like, and always has been like. As God incarnate he showed, through life and death and resurrection, the depth of the Father's love. This was not something new. He did not reveal a 'changed' God, but revealed him in a new light. He revealed, with a new incarnational clarity, the God who is always self-sacrificing and forgiving. He redeemed us from our own illusions. He taught us about God by living God rather than by just talking about him.

Like all of us ever since, the scriptural writers were stuck with the disastrous inadequacy of words. I believe that at the heart of the New Testament is a struggle to communicate the effect that Jesus had had on the writers, and most specifically on the effect that he had had on their relationship with God. Jesus revealed to them a new way to God; he broke down barriers and helped them to find a peace with God that had hitherto eluded them. They were struggling to communicate certain truths about the relationship between God and man – the intersection of anthropology and theology – and in their struggle they often came up with concepts that are closely paralleled in other faith traditions. At the very heart of what I am trying to say in this book is the belief that, although we are not all trying to say the same thing, we are all trying to express the inexpressible, and to explain similar experiences through the medium of a very limited vocabulary.

This is a large claim. Concepts such as salvation do not easily travel into other cultures: indeed, the very concept of eternal (as in everlasting) life is anathema to the average Hindu or Buddhist: salvation to him would be the exact opposite, at least on the surface. But when mere humans, even extremely articulate humans, try to talk about deeply felt spiritual experiences, they are almost inevitably led to a brick wall of inexpressibility. Furthermore, when these experiences are expressed, they are naturally expressed in the terms that the prevailing philosophical thought-worlds of that culture could at least begin to grasp. These then get codified and become dogmas, rather than living expressions of life-changing and life-enhancing experience. And dogmas do not travel well.

Liberation

Right at the heart of all authentic religious experience is the sense of liberation, of being freed from a great weight. In Western traditions this is often defined in terms of sin, and of being rescued from its consequences through the sacrifice of an innocent victim, or by the grace of a merciful God. In Eastern traditions this has more commonly been seen in terms of *Moksa*, of the release from the endless round of birth and rebirth. In both traditions there is the sudden realisation of being valued: in the East this is seen as an escape from transience into permanence and (semi)-divine value; in the West this is seen in terms of being valued by a God who no longer treats our failings as a barrier.

Of course this is a gross over-simplification, and one from a Christian perspective at that, which ignores extensive overlaps between the traditions, but I do not believe that it misses the heart of religious experience. Although the foundation (and other) documents of all faiths have plenty that talk of other areas of religious experience, an insistent voice always seems to echo of liberation, of new and dynamic freedom. It is this experience that Christians call salvation, atonement, redemption, or even forgiveness. Even Christianity cannot find one word to describe the fullness of the experience, despite its relatively homogenous cultural origins in the Greek/Roman/Jewish world of the first century CE. So it is hardly surprising that other faiths, from their vastly different cultural homes, have produced other and more varied models in their attempt to express this inexpressible.

There is here a new relationship with 'the other'. Evelyn Underhill, once of the pioneers of the study of mysticism, pointed out as long ago as 1914 that this commonality of experience is perhaps at its most obvious within the mystical tradition, although certainly not confined to it: 'This unmistakable experience has been achieved by the mystics of every religion, and when we read their statements, we know that all are speaking of the same thing.'[13]

The Jewish Experience

For the Jews, the primary context of this salvation is communal, and based firmly on the covenant relationship that they, as a people, had with the Lord their God. This was the Lord who had saved them from slavery in Egypt,[14] and who had ever since kept a guiding, judgemental and merciful eye over them. This is most frequently expressed in terms of *hesed*, variously translated into English as 'loving-kindness',[15] 'compassion and pity',[16] 'kindness',[17] 'mercy',[18] 'steadfast love',[19] 'everlasting love',[20]

13. Evelyn Underhill, *Practical Mysticism*, London 1914, pages 133-134
14. Exodus 20:2 et passim
15. Psalm 40:11 KLV
16. Exodus 34:6 GNB
17. Joel 2:13 RSV
18. 2 Chronicles 5:13 KJV
19. Psalm 136 passim NRSV
20. Jeremiah 31:3 RSV

amongst others. One modern writer on Judaism has explained it like this:

> Divine mercy is an expression of God's character as Redeemer, 'with whom there is loving-kindness and plenteous redemption'.[21] As Redeemer, his judgments upon individuals and nations for rebelling against him are not vindictive in character. They have, that is to say, as aim the redemption of humanity from its sins, miseries and follies, and its ultimate happiness and salvation.[22]

There is, for the Jew, a real sense of God with us, of God with the chosen people of Israel as a whole, granting of his bounty to his people in order to met their deepest needs. Rabbi Abraham ben Alexander Katz of Kalisk, a Hassidic Rabbi who emigrated with his followers to Palestine in 1777, expressed this hope/experience in terms that echo the Biblical hope, and would have resonated even with those Jews who found some of his teachings a trifle strange: 'God will dwell in their midst, and they will receive from him an abundance of salvation and consolation.'[23]

Yet, this corporate and communal experience of divine forgiveness and redemption can also be experienced at a personal level:

> I look to the Lord for help at all times,
> And he rescues me from danger.
> Turn to me, Lord, and be merciful to me,
> Because I am lonely and weak.
> Relieve me of my worries
> And save me from all my troubles.
> Consider my distress and suffering
> And forgive all my sins.[24]

21. Psalm 130:7
22. Isidore Epstein, *Judaism*, Penguin Books, 1970, page 136
23.Rabbi Abraham ben Alexander Katz of Kalisk (d 1810), quoted in Joseph Weiss, *Studies in Eastern European Jewish Mysticism*, OUP, 1985, page 163
24. Psalm 25:15-18

Then I confessed my sins to You;
I did not conceal my wrong-doings.
I decided to confess them to You,
And You forgave all my sins.[25]

Even though for the Jew there could be no such thing as a soli-
tary salvation, there is a very real sense that what was experienced by the whole community needed to be internalised at a
personal level if it was to become real. Thus Passover was seen
not just as historical celebration of the rescue from Egypt, but as
a reminder of what the Lord did for *me* as an individual when I
came forth from Egypt.

The Experience of Islam

Within Islam the idea that Allah is a forgiving God is absolutely
central. Each Sura (chapter) of the Quran begins with the invoca-
tion 'in the Name of Allah, the compassionate, the merciful.' The
Muslim is intensely aware of the unity, the holiness, the otherness and the greatness of God: this indeed can be seen as the
core of Muhammad's message, reiterated on almost every page
of the Quran. Yet this same God is no remote monad, but the
'oft-forgiving, most merciful',[26] 'the One who accepts repent-
ance from his servants, and forgives sins',[27] the Lord who 'is
ample in forgiveness,'[28] who is always ready to wipe the slate
clean. There is a very real sense within Islam that, since there is
no way that man could ever live up to the demands of the utter
purity of God, then God himself acts in totally characteristic
generousity to accept, forgive and restore his fallen creatures.

There is a Hadith (a tradition concerning Muhammad that
carries a near-canonical status for Muslims) that records: 'Allah
the Almighty has said: O son of Adam, so long as you call upon
me and ask of me, I shall forgive you for what you have done,
and I shall not mind. O son of Adam, were your sins to reach the

25. Psalm 32:5
26. Quran 39:53; (cf 4:110)
27. Quran 42:25
28. Quran 53:32

clouds of the sky, and were you then to ask forgiveness of me, I would forgive you.'[29]

This is an overwhelming sense of the divine forgiveness that is far from unusual:

O God, you are disposed to forgive,
While I am sinful.[30]

Your clemency is greater than my sins.[31]

There is no minor sin when his justice confronts you
And there is no major sin when his grace confronts you.[32]

Within Islam forgiveness is an unmediated gift of God. Its experience is very real, especially during the great Hajj (pilgrimage to Mecca) and the annual fast of Ramadan. The intensity of the feeling of acceptance by God is, perhaps, all the more powerful in a faith which puts such emphasis on the power and unity of God.

The Experience of Hinduism

Within Hinduism salvation (*Moksa*) and forgiveness find a very different cultural and philosophical context. The Indian worldview is governed to a significant extent by the belief in reincarnation – an endless cycle of birth and rebirth whose precise nature depends on the moral quality of the previous life/lives. Salvation is ultimately salvation *from* this everlasting cosmic treadmill into the nearer presence of God.

However, within this context, there is also room for personal forgiveness, a forgiveness that 'is not attained by human merit, but only by the grace of God',[33] and which is available in the

---

29. An-Nawawi No 49, quoted in Owen O'Sullivan, *One God, Three Faiths*, Columba Press, 2002, page 23
30. Kwaja Abdullah Ansari (1006-1089), *Intimate Conversations with God*, trans Thackson, SPCK, 1978, page 192
31. Ibid, page 194
32. Ibn 'Ata 'Illah (-1309) *Kitab al-Hikam* 6:50, trans Danner, SPCK, 1978, page 60
33. John B Chethimattam, *Patterns of Indian Thought*, Geoffrey Chapman, 1971, page 105

here-and-now. This is well illustrated by a verse from the *Bhagavadgita*: 'leave all things behind, and come to me for thy salvation. I will make thee free from the bondage of sins. Fear no more.'[34] The language used in this passage speaks of a personal religious experience conceptualised in language not that far removed from that of Jesus: 'Give thy mind to me, and give me thy heart, and thy sacrifice and thy adoration. This is my Word of promise: thou shalt in truth come to me, for thou art dear to me'[35] – a personal invitation from the incarnate God Krisna that almost pre-echoes Jesus' words: 'Come to me, all ye who labour and are heavy laden, and I will give you rest.'[36]

Moksa is the goal of faith and the gift of God: 'we make ourselves open to the power of God, which God makes available to us. Accepting God's acceptance of us, love answering love – this is also the profound theme of Hindu theism. *This* is liberation.'[37]

The Sikh Experience

To the Sikh Gurus, liberation of various kinds was central to the entire religious quest. It was, firstly, liberation from the endless cycle of birth and rebirth: 'Through the remembrance of the Lord one is freed from rebirth.'[38] But it is more than that: the same liturgical text talks of 'sin's filth being washed away',[39] and elsewhere there is talk of devotees being 'freed from all sorrow, their sufferings ever erased.'[40] Suffering and sin 'must flee from all who hear the Word.'[41] God is seen as 'a God of grace 'who actively communicates the truth that sets men free'.[42] In meditation

---

34. *Bhagavadgita* 18:66, cf 9:1
35. ibid, verse 65
36. Matthew 11:28
37. K.Sivaraman, 'The meaning of Moksha in contemporary Hindu thought and life' in W. Foy, *Man's Religious Quest*, Croom Helm, 1978, page 138
38. Guru Arjan's *Sukhmani* 2:1, in W. H. McLeod, *Textual Sources for the Study of Sikhism*, Manchester University Press, 1984, page 111
39. ibid, page 112
40. ibid, page 50
41. ibid page 87
42. ibid page 40

He who repeats the Name will find himself free.
Hear me, my friend, for I long to hear
The tale which is told in the company of the saved.[43]

The Buddhist Experience

It is harder to find such direct parallels in the non-theistic traditions of Asia – Buddhism, Confucianism and Taoism, amongst
others. The Buddhist seeks enlightenment, a release from transience and suffering through a self-disciplined adherence to the
eightfold path of the Buddha. To the Buddhist – as to many
crypto-Manichean Christians – the created world is *Maya*, illusion, and therefore, logically at least, any salvation has to be salvation outside of this earthly life.

In the Buddhist tradition salvation, enlightenment, is achieved
by knowledge, albeit not knowledge as commonly perceived.
The Buddhist enlightenment is rather a dart of utter comprehension, whereby that which had previously only been known in
the head suddenly descends into the heart at a totally new level
of awareness. This then results in salvation; not salvation in the
sense a Christian might recognise it, conceptualised as atonement or forgiveness, but rather Nirvana – 'a liberation of the real
and eternal self from the empirical self entangled in the sphere
of *Maya* – the real self being thought of as identical with the
Absolute. The storm is over; the tossed and troubled wave sinks
back on the bosom of the unruffled ocean of Eternal Being.'[44]
There is a finality about this Nirvana because its very existence
is in some way a non-existence, incompatible with continued
living in this world of *Maya*.

Despite the huge contextual differences in religious experience, there are also significant areas of overlap. The eleventh
principal of Buddhism, as published by the Buddhist Society of
London, states that 'no man has the right to interfere in his
neighbour's journey to the Goal',[45] thereby accepting that in

---

43. ibid, page 112
44. B. H. Streeter, *The Buddha and the Christ*, Macmillan, 1932, page 284
45. The complete 12 principles of Buddhism are quoted in William
Macquitty, *Buddha*, Thomas Nelson, 1969, page 127

some sense are all moving in the same direction. Buddha and Jesus both show a way of redemption from selfishness and dissatisfaction, different paths that individually 'made sense' in the cultural worlds in which they were and preached. There is also a real sense that, even though Nirvana is not attainable in the here-and-now, there is something in the following of the eightfold path that produces a sense of peace, of wholeness and of integrity not that far removed from similar religious experiences in other, differently conceptualised faith. 'He is like a man freed from debt, or recovered from sickness, or loosed from the bonds of prison, or as a freed slave.'[46] 'Even as the moon makes light in black darkness, so in one moment the supreme bliss removes all defilement.'[47] The contemporary Buddhist, without claiming to have attained either enlightenment or Nirvana, evinces an inner peace and tranquillity, a sense of freedom, that would suggest that what he has experienced in faith is not all that different in its practical reality from what the Christian, Jew or Muslim has also experienced within his or her own faith-world.

Objections

All this may be very well, but it is not proof in any theological, scientific or academic sense. These quotes can equally well be seen as little more than tantalising hints, glimmers of God in other traditions that are appreciated but of little value because they do not fall within the traditional Christian embrace. They are positive, but not salvific because they do not accept Jesus Christ as Lord and Saviour. All they show is that, at certain levels, there is an intersection of experience that transcends formal denominational or credal boundaries.

Some people would regard these glimmers as an Old Testament, as a *preparatio evangelica*, which prepare the soul for the fullness of revelation in Jesus Christ. That approach would

---

46. Edward J. Thomas, *The History of Buddhist Thought*, Routledge and Kegan Paul,1933, 1971 edition, page 120
47. Saraha, *Dohakosha* (9th century), 97 in Conze, *Buddhist texts through the ages*, Bruno Cassirer, 1954, page 237

be a fairly common one in missionary circles, especially in those circles which would regard themselves as enlightened and sympathetic. But such an attitude is really rather patronising, in the same way as Rahner's anonymous Christians thesis is patronising. It is, anyway, rather hard to regard Islam, as the younger faith, as in any way an Old Testament to Christianity.

Yet, in analogy, there is some mileage in this idea, if not the exact term. The (Jewish) Old Testament is full of references to salvation. Most commonly this refers to the events of the Exodus, so it is a physical and historical salvation, rather than a spiritual and eschatological one. Yet, there is still a real confidence, especially in the Psalms, that God will save the individual from a wide range of perils,[48] and grant forgiveness to the penitent sinner.[49] So, for the Christian who accepts the Old Testament as in some manner authoritative, there certainly seems to be some level of salvation available outside the Christian dispensation. This is reinforced by St Paul, who explicitly identifies the rock that was with the Israelites during their wanderings in the wilderness with Christ.[50] So, not only is the work of Christ (namely atonement, salvation and forgiveness) available outside the formal structures, or even faith system of the church, but Christ himself is also present outside the church.

So, Jesus Christ is not limited to the church. Furthermore, he also wills that 'all people be saved'.[51] St John (if he was the author) further extends Christ's work of forgiveness of sin to the entire human race: 'Christ himself is the means by which our sins are forgiven, and not our sins only, but also the sins of everyone.'[52] God's grace, according to the author of Titus, is revealed 'for the salvation of all mankind.'[53] These verses are pointers to the probability that the New Testament writers, despite their insistence on the importance and uniqueness of

48. Psalm 31:5
49. Psalm 51
50. 1 Corinthians 10:4
51. 1 Timothy 2:4
52. 1 John 2:2
53. Titus 2:11

Christ, were also careful not to limit him to the confines of what they understood and preached.

These hints were not allowed to remain unnoticed. As early as 165 AD, Justin Martyr was seeking to 'sell' the Christian faith to the Roman emperor Antoninus Pius, in part by including vast numbers of the seemingly pagan as 'anonymous Christians':

> One article of our faith is that Christ is the First-begotten of God, and we have already proved him to be the very *Logos*, or universal Reason, of which mankind are all partakers; and therefore those who live by reason are in some sort Christians, notwithstanding they may pass with you for atheists. Such among the Greeks were Socrates and Heraclitus ...[54]

The Quaker apologist Robert Barclay (1648-1690) spent a considerable part of his *Apology* (1678) asserting the universal efficacy of Christ's saving death:

> Just as many of the ancient philosophers may have been saved, so may some of those today whom providence has placed in remote parts of the world where the knowledge (of the historical Jesus) is lacking, be made partakers of the divine mystery ... there is an evangelical and saving light and grace in everyone, and the love and mercy of God towards mankind were universal, both in the death of his beloved Son, the Lord Jesus Christ, and in the manifestation of the light in the heart.[55]

As Barclay argues, it is a bit uncharitable to argue that those outside the institutional church cannot be saved.[56] Not only is it a bit uncharitable, it is yet another incidence of our alarming tendency to make a God in our own image: small, mean, petty minded and rule-constrained.

Many representatives of other faith traditions do not seem to

54. Justin Martyr, *Apology LXI*. Undated translation published in London by Griffith, Farran, Okeden and Welsh as part of the Ancient and Modern Library of Theological Literature.
55. Barclay's *Apology*, Proposition 6, in Dean Freiday *Barclay's Apology in Modern English*, Mannasquam, New Jersey, 1967, page 72
56. ibid, page 113

have the same problem. Jews generally seem to be far more relaxed about proselytism and the possibility of a loving God outside their immediate context:

> I certainly believe that he who leads mankind to virtue in this world cannot be damned in the next.[57]

The Doctrine of Universal Salvation is a given within Mahayana Buddhism, and can be seen in the writings of many modern day western Buddhists:

> In my mind, when a Christian mystic deep in prayer or meditation experiences a divine response, when a Pure Land devotee feels the presence of Amitabha or Kuanyin, and when a Ch'an meditator feels Mind respond to mind, all three are visited by an identical experience.[58]

Neither is Islam a closed book on these matters, even though there is little either in the Quran or the tradition that holds out much hope to 'idolaters' or those from outside the Judaeo-Christian Semitic matrix. There is at least some level of hope for the 'People of the Book' (Jews and Christians) who are regarded in the Quran as being 'in the ranks of the righteous'[59] and of whom it is asserted that 'of the good that they do nothing will be rejected of them.'[60]

A mystical experience?
It is not enough just to illustrate the fact that certain people, from certain faiths and at certain times, have believed in the doctrine of universal redemption. They may or may not be representative. Whether they were deluded or onto an important truth depends on similarities of faith experience within and between the faith traditions. We have already seen how, within all faiths, there is a common thread of liberation, variously conceptu-

57. Moses Mendelssohn, *Letter to Johann Caspar Lavatar* (1769), quoted in H. Kupferberg, *The Mendelssohns*, W. H. Allen, 1972, page 36
58. John Blofeld, *Beyond the Gods: Buddhist and Taoist Mysticism*, George Allen and Unwin, 1974, page 160
59. Quran 3:114
60.Quran 3:11

alised. But there are other areas of common experience, particularly amongst those who go loosely under the name 'mystic'.

One such common experience is that of feeling subsumed in God, of being swallowed up in something greater, of unity with the divine. New Testament Christianity, particularly St Paul, sums this up in the phrase being 'in Christ'[61] – a phrase that naturally leads on to the belief that those in Christ are in some manner united with God himself. Those who are united with Christ become one spirit with him,[62] and therefore become one with the Father in whom Jesus mutually indwells.[63] Paul records a 'mystical' experience, where he was taken out of the body, and saw 'many wonderful things'[64] and it is experiences such as this that have been the hallmark of mystical practice down the ages:

No soul can rest until it is detached from all creation.[65]

For by the unceasing and absolute renunciation of thyself and all things thou mayest be borne of high, through pure and entire self-abnegation, into the super-essential radiance of the divine darkness.[66]

Lord, lock me up in the deepest depths of your heart; and then, holding me there, burn me, purify me, set me on fire, sublimate me, till I become utterly what you would have me be, through the utter annihilation of my ego.[67]

The final aim of Torah ... is to attain the perfect *ayin*, wherefore a man should render his self- non-existant.[68]

---

61. e.g. 2 Corinthians 15:17
62. 1 Corinthians 6:17
63. John 14:11
64. 2 Corinthians 12:1-7
65. Julian of Norwich (1342-1416), *Revelations of Divine Love*, trans Wolters, Penguin, 1966, page 68
66. Pseudo-Dionysius (Christian, c 500 AD) *Mystica Theologica 1*, Shrine of Wisdom, 1965, page 9
67. Pierre Teilhard de Chardin (1881-1955) 'The Mass of the World' in *Hymn of the Universe*, Collins, 1970, page 31
68. Rabbi Abraham ben Alexander Katz of Kalisk (died 1810), quoted in Joseph Weiss, *Studies in Easter European Jewish Mysticism,OUP*, page 157

> The sum of their (the Sufis') sciences is the removal of the soul's deficiencies ... so as to achieve a heart empty of all save God, and adorned with the constant remembrance of God.[69]

This mystical experience of detachment from earthly things in order to achieve unity with the divine is also there in Eastern religious experience. For the Hindu, *Moksa* is thought of as a release from the endless round of birth and rebirth through the gradual detaching of the self from earthly attachment and loving devotion to God. For Buddhism, the realisation of the essential non-being of all being, including the self, is an essential part of enlightenment, and although there is no formal concept of a God into whom one can be subsumed, the mystical concept of the divine darkness is not that far removed from the Buddhist concept of non-being. Nirvana has been described, amongst other things, as the cool cave, the place of bliss, emancipation, liberation, the supreme, the transcendent, the calm, the immaterial, the imperishable, the abiding, the supreme joy, the ineffable and the detachment.[70] All of these concepts are ones that have parallels in other faiths. All of them are expressions, both of ultimate truth, but also of the human struggle to find words with which to communicate the intense emotions of the experience of confronting that ultimate truth. In face of that Truth, self becomes less important, even though, paradoxically, one result of the confrontation and self-abnegation may well be the reaffirmation and enrichment of all that is most important in the self.

---

69. Muhammad ibn Muhammad Abu Hamid al-Ghazali (1055-1111), *al-Munqidh min al-dalal,* in N. Calder, J. Majaddedi and A. Rippin, *Classical Islam: a sourcebook of religious literature,* Routledge, 2003, page 229
70. T. W. Rhys Davids, *Early Buddhism,* page 71. Quoted in Edward J. Thomas, op. cit., page 120

CHAPTER 4

The Self-Revelation of God

He is, so we must understand him.[1]

If God is to speak his Word to the soul, it must be still and at peace, and then he will speak his Word and give himself to the soul.[2]

Holy Scriptures

The written word plays a vitally important role in all the world's major religions, although its exact status varies considerably between and even within faiths. At one end of the spectrum are those who believe that their sacred book or books are the actual words of God, infallible down to the smallest detail. At the other end of the same spectrum we find those for whom their scriptures are little more than time-hallowed devotional reading. For almost all religious people, particularly those within the Judaeo-Christian-Islamic family of faiths, their scriptures are, at very least, a primary source of their knowledge of God, a vital foundation document that informs and structures their religious experience and their knowledge of God. And so, in this chapter, it is with the written scriptural Word that our discussion of the divine self-revelation must begin.

To the Muslim, the Quran is revealed 'by Allah, the exalted in power, full of wisdom',[3] and is universally regarded as the uncreated and infallible Word of God. There would be many within the Christian faith, particularly those of an evangelical persuasion, who would hold the Bible in comparably high esteem, and many more who could give their assent to the 39 Articles of the Anglican Church: 'Holy Scripture containeth all

---

1. Katha Upanishad 6:13
2. Sermon 1, in *Meister Eckhart – a modern translation,* trans R. B. Blakney, Harper and Row, 1941, page 99
3. Quran 45:2

things necessary to salvation',[4] or, as Vatican Council II would have it, 'God's own Word in unalterable form.'[5]

In many Churches, particularly in the Roman Catholic, Orthodox and Anglo-Catholic traditions, this high regard for scripture is liturgically underlined by the gospel procession, in which the Bible is carried into the body of the congregation, and often censed, for the reading of the gospel. This veneration of the physical presence of the Bible is commonplace: 'Every Catholic home should possess a Bible. Every family should read it. It would be impressive and natural, indeed, to find the Bible open and in an honoured place in every Catholic home, placed open perhaps on a table or a stand, with a light burning occasionally before it.'[6]

To the Jews, their Torah is an altogether more exalted entity: 'its content and connotations embrace more than "religion" or "creed" alone, or "ethics" or "commandments" or "learning" alone, and it is not even just a combination of all these, but something far transcending all of them. It is a mystic, almost cosmic conception. The Torah is the tool of the creator; with it and for it he created the universe. The Torah is older than the creation. It is the highest idea and living soul of the world. Without it the world could not exist and would have no right to exist.'[7]

Within Hinduism and Buddhism the situation is far more fluid, with a vast body of sacred texts at least six times as long as the Christian Bible, regarded as having divine authority, and as being 'revealed' and 'heard'. They are a far less coherent corpus than either Christian, Jewish or Islamic scriptures, but this is a multiplicity and diversity that does not bother adherents of either faith. Yet they have given rise to a multiplicity of

---

4. Article 6 of the 39 Articles
5. *Dei Verbum* 21, 18 November 1965, in Flannery (ed), *Vatican II, The Conciliar and Post Conciliar Documents*, Dominican Publications. Dublin, 1981, page 762
6. Cahal Daly, then bishop of Down and Dromore, *Message to his people*, 11 May 1986.
7. H. N. Bailik, in A. Hertzberg (ed), *Judaism*, Prentice Hall, 1961 page 85

'schools', with a multiplicity of theologies, all regarding these texts as in some sense inspired and divine.

While I would agree with all these that scripture is of absolutely central importance, I do find a scriptural fundamentalism of any sort rather difficult. Such fundamentalism, I find, rather limits the power and scope of the written word, insisting on a self-authenticating consistency when no consistency was intended. Such fundamentalism all too often tips over into legalism, and insists that there is only one valid interpretation of the words. It can become a straitjacket, one within which folk are afraid to let their religious imagination run free. I would prefer to see scripture as a codification of the early primal enthusiasm of the faith community which gave that faith its initial impulse and meaning, an inspired expression of faith, purpose, direction and joy, a 'glorious keepsake' from the divine.[8] They are a written place in which God may be discerned, an enormously rich repository of inherited wisdom and primitive grace. In them 'we are not simply coming to a document which directs and legislates, but to a dramatic focus of religious experience to which we must respond.'[9] Scriptures are 'the map we need to make the journey, but they are not the journey itself, any more than the menu is the actual meal'.[10]

Scripture points to God, like a menu to a meal or a signpost to our destination. There is a real danger in fundamentalism that the written words of the book itself become of such heightened importance that they actually obscure God. A living faith needs to look beyond the written word to the incarnate Word (to use Christian terminology and experience); it needs even to look beyond incarnate Word to the God made manifest by both incarnation and written word. Scripture is only part of the self-revelation of God; we limit both God and the scriptures we claim to venerate if we are so focused on them that we fail to see them as

8. Kwaja Addullah Ansari, *Intimate Conversations with God,* ed and trans W. M. Thackston, SPCK, 1979, page 194

9. Kenneth Cragg, *The Christ and the Faiths: Theology in Cross-reference,* SPCK , 1986, page 63

10. Alan Jones, *Living the Truth,* Cowley Publications, 2000, page 35

only a pointer. Words and language are, by their very nature, symbols that communicate beyond themselves: they are finite; God is infinite.

There is an old story, told once by Anthony de Mello, of a man who left his village to visit Mumbai. He walked for many days, until he came to the sign at the edge of that great conurbation that heralded the fact that he had arrived at last. So he looked at the sign; he walked round the sign; he fondled the sign; he even slept the night under the sign before leaving the next day to return to his village. He mistook the sign for the reality.

Scripture is a sign, it is one of the many pointers that show the ways of God and the way to God. When we travel, we do not look at the map or the compass all the time – otherwise we would never see where we were going, and would crash. We would also miss the beauties along the roadside. Scripture, like a map, is a sign, and is there to be referred to, to give us a sense of direction, a sense of place, a structure within which to place and understand our religious world. It is a map that tells us, amongst other things, where we can find God. It is not, and never can be, a living world in itself. 'Because the scriptures themselves are only a declaration of the source, and not the source itself, they are not to be considered the principal foundation of all truth and knowledge. They are not even to be considered as the adequate primary rule of faith and practice.'[11] That is not their nature.

There are further problems for those who would be fundamentalists. The world has changed immeasurably since these ancient texts were first spoken and put to parchment. The culture in which they were formed (and within which they were first revealed) had been lost forever. We read texts, and hear words, in a vastly different way. Our expectations and our thought-world are completely different. The world in which the scriptures of all faiths were written was pre-scientific and pre-Enlightenment. So if we begin to take account of the vast differ-

---

11. Robert Barclay, Apology (1676), trans Dean Freiday, Manasquan New Jersey, 1980, page 46

ences between that world and the world of today (as I believe
we should) we have to move away from fundamentalism. If we
do not take these things into account, we risk making scripture
seem out-dated, or forcing much of it into a meaning that was
never intended by the authors.

Also, particularly for Christians and Jews, there is a huge difficulty in ascertaining the correct form of the text as it has become corrupted over the years, and many different versions and
translations have come down to us, even from very early times.
This is, of course, the criticism that Islam likes to level at Jewish
and Christian texts.[12] Editorial notes such as 'the meaning of the
Hebrew is uncertain', 'the text of this verse is uncertain', 'the
Hebrew of v 29-33 is obscure'[13] litter scholarly translations of the
Bible. Under these circumstances, how can we possibly be fundamentalists, unless we are very selective in what we choose to
regard as worthy of our fundamentalism.

Within Christianity selective fundamentalism is rife. I am
probably guilty of it myself on occasion. But then I have yet to
meet a professed fundamentalist who actually maintains a
rigourous and consistent fundamentalism. Every religious person can amen verses such as 'Do not take revenge on anyone or
continue to hate him, but love your neighbour as yourself.'[14]
They are good, sensible words that speak of a well-ordered society and of high ethical values. But I have yet to meet anyone
who is similarly enthusiastic about the very next verse: 'Do not
crossbreed domestic animals. Do not plant two kinds of seed in
the same field. Do not wear clothes made of two different kinds
of material.'[15] I have yet to meet anyone who seriously proposes
that we should continue to stone adulterers[16] or those who gather

12. Muhammad Rida al-Muzaffer, *The Faith of Shi'a Islam*, The
Muhammadi Trust, 1982, page 23
13. all footnotes from the book of Job in the RSV
14. Leviticus 19:18
15. Leviticus 19:19
16. Deuteronomy 22:2

firewood on the Sabbath.[17] Few still buy into the Old Testament acceptance of polygamy,[18] slavery and concubinage.[19]

Scripture is vastly more complex and rich than simple fundamentalism would allow. There are even apparent contradictions (which I would prefer to call creative tensions) such as the disagreement between the Ten Commandments and the prophet Ezekiel: 'I will bring punishment on those who hate me down to the third and fourth generation';[20] 'A son is not to suffer because of his father's sins, nor a father because of the sins of his son.'[21] Or take the widely held belief in Deuteronomic and Wisdom circles that 'the Lord will not let good people go hungry, but he will keep the wicked from getting what they want',[22] of which the writer of Ecclesiastes said: 'This is nonsense. Look at what happens in the world: sometimes righteous men get the punishment of the wicked, and the wicked men get the reward of the righteous.'[23]

I could go on, but the primary purpose of this chapter is not to debunk fundamentalism. This has been done at greater length and with far greater scholarship by the likes of James Barr.[24] It is, rather, to prise open the phenomenon of the self-revelation of God, to discern how God is revealed through the scriptures. Scripture is vital and positive, if correctly handled. If we overrate it, we can begin to feel inadequate when certain parts of it definitely do not speak to us. We can indulge in ostrich-like behaviour when we studiously ignore or seek to explain away those passages that fit awkwardly with our pre-conceived notions of how we should relate to the sacred text. If we under-rate it, on the other hand, we run the equally serious risk of dismissing the wisdom of the ancients and of shutting our eyes to what

17. Numbers 15:35
18. Leviticus 18:8, Deuteronomy 12:30
19. Leviticus 19:20
20. Exodus 20:5
21. Ezekiel 18:20
22. Proverbs 10:3
23. Ecclesiastes 8:14
24. James Barr, Fundamentalism, SCM, 1981

has always been used by God as a vehicle of his self-communication.

In this sense, scripture is like doctrine. We need it as a framework and guide. We need it to contextualise and structure what
we believe. We need it to authenticate our religious experience.
But we must not let it rule and control. We must read it with our
minds, with a faith that seeks to understand.

So, then, how does God reveal himself through scripture if
that scripture is not the *ipsissima vox dei*?[25]

He reveals himself most obviously in passages that speak to
the individual's needs at a particular time in life. We are more
likely to be susceptible to particular passages when we are in a
state of heightened emotional need, such as bereavement or
chronic illness. He speaks when we open ourselves to hear his
voice. He speaks when we are gathered with other like-minded
folk, meeting to discuss what scripture has to say. He speaks
when the sheer poetry of the text can transport us far beyond the
words. He speaks when scripture relates the involvement of
God in the life of the saints and in the history of his people, and
especially when the tale of that involvement resonates with our
own situation.

He speaks: that very phase is charged, because speaking suggests words, and divine Word suggests authority, which in turn
suggests law. It is logically valid to see scripture in this way, and
to believe that all its words are charged with meaning and authority. However, it is not the only logically valid way of looking at it, for in religious tradition word is creative, it is calming,
it is balm. The Word of God sustains and nurtures us and – in
the Christian scheme at least – becomes incarnate, becomes vul-
nerable, becomes inadequate.

So, in this scheme of things, scripture ceases to be law and becomes a springboard, a trampoline to freedom, to an intensely
personal alertness to God. It becomes 'a lamp to our feet'[26] and

25 The literal word of God.
26. Psalm 119:105

'a light by which ye shall walk'.[27] Its stories become our story, its poems our poems and it opens the world to us in a new way so that the whole of creation becomes charged with the grandeur of God. We become imbued with the spirit of scripture, with the Spirit behind scripture, somehow becoming closer to the creation, to ourselves, and to God. This is a subjective thing, at least in part – but somehow it is more than subjective, in that it allows us to become part of a long tradition of God-awareness. The resonances of old find meaning for the here-and-now; the scriptural cadences help us to make sense of what we see, and place us in unbroken line with hallowed folk of old. We develop a sense of belonging, both to the world, and to a deeply rooted community of faith. And that is immensely satisfying.

But even as that is true, and scripture proves to be immensely uplifting, there will always be parts of it that remain lifeless, and there will always be days when we are just not feeling open to its majesty. Passages such as the genealogies of Matthew or the long name lists of Ezra and Nehemiah are prosaic, to say the least. And there are other passages that are downright abhorrent, such as the assertion that the sons of Levi consecrated themselves 'as priests in the service of the Lord by killing your sons and brothers, so the Lord has given you his blessing.'[28] Maybe it is a failing on my part, but the historical and cultural gap is just too great for me to find that anything other than ghastly. God does not speak to me in that passage, save by strengthening my resolve to ensure that such religious extremism cannot be allowed to degrade our world ever again.

My use of scripture is selective, but I hope honestly so. There are parts of it that I cannot amen, in any tradition; there are parts of it to which I cannot say that 'this is the Word of the Lord' – yet those passages are the shadows against which the positive parts are set, the all-too-human bits that underscore the prevailing power of the rest. I make no attempt to put the whole of scrip-

27. Quran 57:28
28. Exodus 32:29

ture on an equal pedestal, but I do hope that, even in its darkest places, I have the humility to let God communicate to me.

And that is the key. Openness to God. That is a frame of mind that needs to extend way beyond scripture. God, if he is to be worthy of that name, must be infinitely more vast than scripture could ever tell, and must be itching to communicate himself in myriad other ways. Different people are temperamentally open to different channels of grace: for some, scripture may be the paramount means; for others poetry, literature, music or one of the other arts. Some may sense the numinous in the amazing discoveries of science, others in the world of nature, and yet others in the humdrum experiences of daily life. For each faith community their own scriptural canon, their own faith tradition, is the filter through which these intimations of the divine are filtered. They make the scriptural page into something experiential, into something which contextualises life-experience.

Literature

Poetry does not speak to everyone, and even within the poetic corpus different folk have different tastes. The appreciation of poetry is something intensely personal: to some Helen Steiner Rice is deeply moving, while others (more intellectually snooty) regard her as a purveyor of cheap sentimental drivel. To others John Donne, Andrew Marvel and Gerald Manley Hopkins communicate something marvellous of God: while to many their works are just too dense and complex. Poetry doesn't even have to be specifically religious to strike a religious chord: when poetry is powerful and begins to transcend its own words, then it is speaking a language akin to that used by religious folk as they search for meaning. As the Quran has so succinctly put it, 'a goodly word is like a goodly tree whose root is firmly fixed and its branches reach to the heavens.'[29] Goodly words – the best words in the best order[30] – is as good a working definition of poetry as I have come across.

---

29. Quran 14:24
30. Samuel Taylor Coleridge, in a letter dated 12 July 1827

Coleridge felt that 'no man was ever yet a great poet without being a profound philosopher';[31] and Matthew Arnold felt that 'genuine poetry is conceived and composed in the soul'.[32] These men may exemplify the romantic tradition in poetry, and their ideals may not be universally recognised, but they have here hit on a fundamental truth of poetry – that it has a spiritual and philosophical dimension (which as far as the ancients were concerned were one and the same thing) beyond words. Poetry has hidden depths of meaning that are often beyond what even the poet recognised at the time of composition: that is why, at its best, its reading can become a quasi-religious experience.

It is one thing for poetry to stir the soul. Secular poetry can only become 'religious' (a thought that might well appal its authors) if the 'religious' sensitivities it awakens find a structure within which to take shape and find meaning. Thus the same words of poetry can inspire different people very differently, and impel them each in their own way to explore very different faith traditions. Someone from a Christian background reading Wordsworth is most likely, if the religious response is awakened, to find that response taking a Christian form; a Muslim or a Baha'í is equally likely to be inspired to return to his or her own faith roots by the same poem.

Equally, poetry can challenge us to consider totally new religious directions: consider how Paul uses quotations from the pagan Athenian poets Epimenides and Aratus as quasi-scriptural texts for his evangelical address to the Areopagus.[33]

Thus poetry, if it is 'religious' at all, is only a general revelation of God, a prompt that encourages the reader to experience something beyond him or herself and then locate that primal urge in a particular religious context. It is rarely – outside specifically religious verse written specifically within and for one tradition, such as Christian hymnody – more focused. Poetry can inspire us God-ward: we then research God within a reli-

---

31. Samuel Taylor Coleridge, *Bibliographia Literaria*, (1817), chap 15
32. Matthew Arnold, *Essays in Criticism*, Thomas Gray.
33. Acts 17:28

gious tradition that gives shape and structure to our poetically inspired yearnings. Spirit speaks to spirit in verse. God sends out an invitation in great (or otherwise moving) poetry, an invitation that is for many the impetus that leads to the renewal of previously lost faith. It isn't scriptural; it has no authority – but it can have power.

'Great literature is simply language charged with meaning to the utmost possible degree.'[34] If there is any truth in this comment, then other forms of writing should also have similar effects to those occasioned by a successful poem: the powerful novel, like any great art, can open up new ways of seeing things that we had not previously considered. It does it differently, of course, using words in a more familiar manner than poetry. But through scenarios, conversation and observation it can open up new perspectives on reality. Great novels, such as those of the Russian masters Dostoyevsky and Tolstoy, illumine the human condition to a searing and challenging depth. In so doing they touch on that intersection between anthropology and theology that is at the heart of the religious quest. In understanding something more about ourselves, we understand God a little bit better. Or, to put it in a more Hindu turn of phrase, in being granted an insight into our own soul we are also granted an insight into the nature of *Atman*, the universal soul.

This, of course, could be accused of being somewhat élitist. Most people do not read 'great literature', but are content with the latest heavily-marketed pot-boiler if they read at all. People read to escape or fill their time while sitting in an aircraft or sunbathing on the beach. Yet even here a laugh is provoked, and a smile creeps occasionally onto the lips as a different world is encroached upon. It may be a shallow world; it may even be a tawdry world, but the very act of entering that world, of willingly suspending our disbelief for a while, moves us beyond where we are. We are taken out of ourselves, we find space, we relax. All these things are good for us, they de-stress us, they take us into a world where we are not number one. That, although not

34. Ezra Pound, *How to Read* (1931), part ii

exactly a religious experience, has parallels with religious experience and can indeed be a preparation for it, God speaking
silently to us to ready us for himself.

This may not be a conscious process. It is more like God soft-
ening up the edges of our sensibilities; a *preparatio evangelica* that
makes us open to a fuller encounter at a later date. But light is
shed, new shards of understanding penetrate our consciousness, and God is there as a still small voice, even though we may
not be able to name him yet.

I don't think that I am arguing that God speaks through all
literature, let alone all writing, although that is theoretically possible for the omnipotent God. In Old Testament times God used
some pretty unsavoury characters – including the Persian
Emperor Cyrus,[35] the original butcher of Baghdad – to fulfil his
purposes. Some literature is, frankly, so pornographic, degrad-
ing and abusive that I find it hard to see God using it except to
plead through its very vileness to our better selves. The person
who is reading such writing is, most probably, doing it in such a
frame of mind that (s)he is less than likely to be open to uplifting
and improving things, (s)he is putting up huge barriers to anything good, and is hardly likely to be open to God, unwittingly
or otherwise. In circumstances such as these God surely can
communicate, but we are not listening. The theoretical possibility
that 'Thy glory is declared even in that which denies thee'[36] remains; it does happen, but perhaps it needs the eye of faith to
discern it.

The Arts

Much the same arguments apply to the visual arts of sculpture
and painting. There is no limit to the communicability of God,
but there are limits as to our receptability. At their best the visual
arts show us things we might otherwise have missed and give
us fresh ways of looking at reality. The Mona Lisa can appear to

---

35. Isaiah 45:1
36. T. S. Eliot, *Murder in the Cathedral*, part II in *The Complete Poems and
Plays of T. S. Eliot*, Faber, 1969, page 281

look diagonally straight at us and mock our pretentiousness with her ridiculous smile. Christ from the cross can challenge, welcome and criticise us when painted with the intensity of an artist such as Grünewald, Rembrandt, Velázques or Van Dyck. But equally, by showing us new ways of looking, even sculpture and painting of a totally secular subject matter and intent – such as some of Henry Moore's nudes or Picasso's *Guernica* – can alert us to the hidden depths and unexpected form of things.

Within the world of Islam, representative art is frowned upon, and in some cases totally banned. Yet the ornate calligraphy of the Quranic texts gives physical beauty to the poetic and spiritual beauty of the written word (as in any illuminated religious manuscript from Ireland through Ethiopia to India and beyond). The intricate, elegant and infinitely flexible geometric patterns that decorate Istanbul's Blue Mosque and the King's Mosque at Isfahan are deliberately designed to lead the mind to the order and mathematical genius of the entire cosmos, and thereby to the Creator himself. Beauty shows us something of God: 'Islamic art, although dealing with the world of forms is, like all genuine religious art, a gate towards the inner life … beauty is the inward dimension of goodness and leads to that reality which is the origin of both beauty and goodness.'[37]

In India and much of the East art is seen primarily in religious terms, as a spur to meditation. It is deliberately religious, and the exact opposite to Islamic art in that it is flamboyant in its depiction of form, both human and divine. It is easy to dismiss such art as idolatry, but that is not its intention. The stone carving of Krishna is not Krishna, but a representation of Krishna that reminds the viewer of the stories concerning him, and of the great texts associated with his name, such as the *Bhagavadgita*. Art provokes religious thinking in the Eastern World.

As with literature, there is much art that is more kitsch than art. Into this category falls much religious art: you only have to glance at the souvenir stalls at any centre of pilgrimage to the see most uninspiring displays of religious art imaginable. Yet this same kitsch, as the cognoscenti would view it, is hugely popular, and hangs in living rooms and from car mirrors throughout the world. This is perhaps more for what it symbolises than for the intrinsic quality of the art itself. But it is viewed as art, and is used to draw the mind of the person looking at it to higher things. Even bad art can be a channel along which folk can move towards God, and God towards them. If God relied on 'high art' he would probably be forgotten by now.

These same arguments can also be applied to music, that 'higher revelation than all wisdom and philosophy.'[38] Music, like silence, is of its nature beyond words, although it often accompanies and enhances words. It can communicate when words are inadequate or inaudible. Yet, like the other arts, it is an intensely personal thing. I find that Bach and Biber, Haydn and Handel, Shostakovich and Schubert (amongst others) all speak to me in almost whatever mood I am in. They have all, in their own way, responded to the numinous. They are the composers I love. If I am in the appropriate fame of mind their music can lead me on beyond myself into a state akin to meditation or prayer: at the very least into a state of contended ease. But, in a different mood their works are just music. Great music, but on that occasion communicating remarkably little.

To me one of the supreme works of western music is Bach's B Minor Mass. Two friends of mine would disagree: on different occasions both of them have come into the room when I was enraptured and enquired as to the nature of the 'ghastly noise' I was listening to. Music is like any of the arts – it communicates through an individual's conscious and unconscious experiences, through their culture and through their mindset. So tastes will vary enormously, through the vast swathes of the European symphonic tradition to the Italian madrigalists; from the hypnotic mantras of rap to the amazing cadences of the Malian Kora or Malagasy Valiha. The possibilities are endless and, although I

38. Ludwig van Beethoven, quoted in Bettina von Armin, *Letter to Goethe* (1810).

personally find it hard to see how anyone can be positively brought beyond themselves by some types of modern music I have to recognise that, for the most part, music is a prime means of the divine self-communication, of opening up an individual to something beyond themselves. That is why most religious traditions have used music in their worship and meditation (Islam being a notable, although not completely consistent, exception).

Others find 'resources for a Secular Theology'[39] in areas such as film or the adrenalin rush of sport. But these areas are not my scene. Besides, the point is already made: the avenues along which God can come and touch us are legion. And they are usually unexpected.

Revelation through nature

But all these are human creations; 'where God appears from the depths',[40] perhaps, but not directly the work of God. The world around us is another matter and a frequent source of wonder and inspiration to both religious and secular folk alike. To the secular mind the cosmos is magnificent, mind-boggling, amazing, a source of wonder; to the religious mind it is all these things and more: it is the 'art of God',[41] for 'the whole universe reflecteth his glory.'[42] 'Heaven and earth and all that they contain proclaim that I should love you.'[43] To the Hindu, the goal of faith is to 'love me (Krishna) in whatever he sees',[44] to respond to the God-in-creation mirrored in the world around. To the Muslim, 'virgin nature is the testament of God.'[45]

Wonder at creation and its fecundity is a fundamental urge behind the religious quest. It seems, for instance, to be the start-

39. Alex Wright, *Why bother with theology?* DLT, 2002
40. Hans Küng, *On being a Christian*, trans Quin, Collins, 1977, page 80
41. Thomas Browne, *Religio Medici* (1643) i
42. *Gleaning from the Writings of Bahá'u'lláh*, trans Shogi Effendi, Baha'í Publishing Trust, 1976, page 166
43. St Augustine of Hippo, *Confessions x.6*, trans Pine Coffin, Penguin, 1961, page 211
44. Bhagavadgita 6:31
45. Seyyid Hosein Nasr, op. cit., page 196

ing point for most Sikh thinking about God: 'There is one God, Eternal trust is his name, creator of all things and the all-pervading spirit.'[46] Fruit and flowers are frequently found as motifs in the earliest temples, as in Solomon's Temple at Jerusalem.[47] It seems as though El Elyon (God Most High), the name for God most associated with Jerusalem, was very much a creator God, to be worshipped because he had 'made heaven and earth'.[48] 'The most prominent gods throughout the history of ancient Egypt in some way represented the power of creation.'[49] And in many faiths there is at least an awareness of God the provider at harvest time, an endless source of gratitude and dependency.[50]

Within some faiths, this sense of wonder is translated into the worship – or placation – of nature spirits. In others, there is a pantheistic sense that God is not just in everything, but that everything is part of God. Yet, within most of the great religious traditions there is a realisation that pantheism is not enough: 'The world is only a partial manifestation of the Godhead, it is not that Divinity. The Godhead is infinitely greater than any natural manifestation can be.'[51] The religious person, although moved to awe by the wonders of creation, hears those very wonders say 'we are not your God; seek what is above us.'[52] God is Spirit, invisible to the naked eye, and because of this 'God cannot be inspected, so the universe we inhabit must provide the data.'[53]

This sense of God-in-his-creation, this semi-philosophical deduction of facts-about-God from the nature of the world he

46. *The Mool Mantra* in *The Sikhs, their religious beliefs and practice*, W. Owen Cole and Piara Singh Sambhi, RKP, 1978, page 69
47. 1 Kings 7:40-49
48. Genesis 14:19, 22
49. Veronica Ions, *Egyptian Mythology*, Paul Hamlyn, 1968, page 20
50. Psalm 67:6,7; Deuteronomy 16:9ff
51. Sri Aurobundo Ghose (1875-1950), *Essays on the Gita 2,I,9*, in Parrinder, *Themes for living: Man and God*, Hulton Educational Publications, 1973, page 56
52. St Augustine of Hippo, *Confessions x.6*, trans Pine Coffin, Penguin, 1961, page 212
53. Helen Oppenheimer, *Making Good*, SCM, 2001, page 48

created and sustains, is a constant theme in literature.
Wordsworth, in his contemplation of the scene around Tintern
Abbey was moved to write:

> And I have felt
> A presence that disturbs me with the joy
> Of elevated thoughts; a sense sublime
> Of something far more deeply interfused,
> Whose dwelling is the light of setting suns,
> And the round ocean, and the living air,
> And the blue sky, and in the mind of man:
> A motion and a spirit, that impels
> All thinking things, all objects of thought
> And rolls though all things.[54]

Wordsworth 'felt a presence', a numinousity in the world about
him: he had the romantic/religious alertness to that-which-is-
beyond, to the sense of 'the other' that is at the core of all spirituality. This is frequently taken a step further, especially by poets
of a mystical bent:

> To see the world in a grain of sand
> And heaven in a wild flower
> Hold infinity in the palm of your hand
> And eternity in an hour.[55]

When folk are close to the natural world, that world is seen in a
new light. I know for myself, as I walk the dog through the seasons in the woodlands around Belfast, that winter trees, bare of
leaves, become sculptured icons of the living God; springtime
speaks of new life, of resurrection, as the bluebells push themselves up through the leaf-mould and the trees burst into bud-
ded life; summers speak of fecundity and vibrant growth, and
autumn of mellow beauty, of giving and ripe beauty. The natural
world becomes a numinous world, charged with the grandeur
of God through which that same God touches me in my inmost
being.

54. Worsdworth, *Tintern Abbey*, 93-102
55. William Blake, *Auguries of Innocence 1* (Poems from the Pickering
Fragment 1803)

This could be called a 'natural religion', a creation-centred spirituality which could very easily become amorphous and 'new-agey'. If grounded in a faith tradition, on the other hand, it can become a spur to the rediscovery of religious truth; it can become the foundation of a religious experience that rejuvenates the tired dogmas that had previously alienated. The 'sense of God' that we get from contemplating his creation authenticates and is authenticated by our various scriptures and traditions. These reinforce each other so that neither is read in isolation, neither is merely subjective, neither is self-authenticating. Scripture and my religious tradition contextualise and to some extent define my experience. But the fit is not absolute: the passage of time and the variety of human experience mean that for each person the outworking of the two will be different. God will come to each along different although possibly parallel paths: some will have met him in the full blast of his glory,[56] others in the still small voice[57] and yet others will have only been granted a tantalising glimpse of his hind-parts![58]

Revelation through science
Scientists seek for greater precision, for theses that most adequately explain the given facts. To some scientists, there is nothing more than science, the empirical study of phenomena. To others, 'religion and science are the two conjugated faces or phases of one and the same act of complete knowledge.'[59]

In many ways science and theology are parallel disciplines, the one reflecting on the encounter with the physical world and the other reflecting on the encounter with God. They both seek objectively to understand reality. They both need data, and they both need faith in the fact that such reflection is worthwhile and possible. Both are confronted with data that at one and the same time exhibits both simplicity and complexity. The scientist is

---

56. Ezekiel chapter 1
57. 1 Kings 19:12
58. Exodus 33:23
59. Teilhard de Chardin, *The Phenomenon of Man*, page 285

faced with the physical world and seeks to understand it. The religious person, theologian or not, has a similar spur in his quest to understand the Divine: 'He is, so we must understand him.'[60]

On one level the scientific enterprise, where it abuts on theological revelation, is a refinement of natural theology: a sense of amazement at the physical world leading to a belief in the One who is the first cause of that physical world. From creation to Creator. But there is more to it than this: scientific discovery is sometimes accompanied by a *eureka* moment, a flash of insight that seems to point to a dimension of reality beyond the everyday.[61] And that, undoubtedly, has parallels in the world of religious experience.

Science is full of theora and laws, often stated in mathematical formulæ that mean little to the uninitiated. In the Christian world statements of faith are similarly made in highly compact creedal formulæ that are also virtually incomprehensible to the outsider. Credal and scientific formulæ are both statements of the order apparent in the world: they are similar in kind and can engender similar security and excitement.

Yet formulæ such as these are not set in stone: they are revisable when new evidence emerges. They can be fine tuned. They are only of value if they are recognised as being different from the reality they seek to explain. They are a veiled explanation only fully comprehensible to the few.[62]

Underneath the seeming certainty of the world of equations, laws and creeds there is a world of flux. Within science that is perhaps best illustrated by the whole concept of quantum mechanics, a world of theory that seeks to make sense of the seeming incompatibility of certain observed phenomena – such as the fact that light can simultaneously display characteristics of both wave and particle. To the uninitiated it is almost impenetrably technical, but it is the best attempt so far to explain the evidence, just as the seeming contradictions of the doctrine of the Trinity are the best stab to date at explaining the nature of God.

60. Katha Upanishad 6:13
61. John Polkinghorne, *Reason and Reality*, SPCK, 1991, page 58
62. 2 Corinthians 3:14

Quantum theory seeks to explain the interconnected and elusive character of the physical world. It has brought about an extension of the limits of what is conceivable. Our imaginations have been enlarged by it.[63] 'In Quantum Theory physics is revealed as having a good deal in common with theology as the latter pursues its search for understanding of the Unpicturable.'[64]

Quantum Theory has pushed scientists to engage in some lateral thinking in order to get behind their ostensibly accurate observations and measurements to a truer understanding of the nature of matter and the forces of nature. It has opened up a whole new world. For some this is fascinating in itself; for others it has been a dual revelation, both of new scientific insight, and into

The Master Mind, the Mind Divine
Which caused the earth to move
To grow, evolve,
Through prayer and praise
To better days
And God.[65]

Quantum theory is only one example of how, for some, the discoveries of science have converged with their understanding of theology, and have reinforced their awareness of how, within this fluctuating yet stable world, God can be discerned. Quantum theory, despite all its precision, is ultimately a symbol – just like all God-talk – and one that forces us into an attitude of humility. 'Blessed is he who has reached the ignorance that is inexhaustible'[66] could be the motto of scientist and theologian alike.

Revelation through human experience
All that has been said so far in this chapter could, in one sense or

63. John Polkinghorne, op. cit., page 86
64. John Polkinghorne, *One World*, SPCK, 1986, page 47
65. Timothy Kinahan, *A More Excellent Way*, Corrymeela Press, 1998, page 125
66. Evagrius of Pontus (346-399) *Gnostic Chapters* iii:8 quoted in A. Louth, *The Origins of the Christian Mystical Tradition*, OUP, 1983, page 108

another, be subsumed under the heading of 'experience'. We have an experience that is mind-blowing, be it a moment of scientific discovery, a sudden unexplained awareness of a deeper reality, a simple contemplation of beauty. Religious theories, religious doctrine, religious scripture, formal revelation have no meaning if they do not relate in some way to such human experiences. We need to have been touched by 'the other' if these things are to have anything other than theoretical significance. 'Revelation presupposes a meaningful human event, an event which is already relevant in human terms without direct reference to God.'[67] It is through experience that God primarily relates to people. That is his Primary Revelation. Only secondly does he resort to formal, or Secondary Revelation, in order to schematise and make sense of what has already been experienced. Scripture is this revelation. It is the faith community's agreed repository of wisdom, interpreted in many different ways yet agreed to be a normative yardstick by which experience is measured, and from which experience gains its wider meaning.

Edward Schillebeeckx talks of how secular events – ordinary experiences of meaning – become 'material of the Word of God.'[68] The formal revelation gives shape and meaning to the seemingly random and amorphous 'religious' experiences of life. What was once mere serendipity becomes an alertness to the presence of God in the unexpected; what was once no more than a significant event becomes revelatory because in it we were aware that something/someone greater than ourselves was operative. For those who do not a have a religious framework within which to make sense of such events, they can just fade away into the history book of memorable moments. But for those who do have such a religious framework, or who take the trouble to search out such a religious framework, these events become charged with the presence of God. They feed into the

67. Edward Schillebeeckx, *Jesus in our Western Culture*, trans Bowden, SCM, 1987, page 11
68. Edward Schillebeeckx, op. cit., page 10

complex equation of life-in-the-context-of-God, and help to ensure that that equation is not lost in either formalism or mean-
inglessness. Formal revelation and serendipitous moments
(Secondary and Primary Revelation respectively) reinforce each
other and make God real.

These experiences can be either corporate or individual. The
corporate experience of 'the other' comes about most obviously
in an act of worship: when a group of Quakers are sitting together
in their meeting house, waiting to hear the Inner Voice; when in
the Hajj millions of Muslims are moving in unison around the
Ka'aba in Mecca; when in a Hindu Temple people begin to chant
together a sacred Mantra, or a church full of Methodists burst
out together in a rousing Wesleyan hymn; when a congregation
are gathered together in eucharistic celebration; when a group of
ancient Israelites went up together to Jerusalem to share in the
worship of Sion.[69] The list of possible scenarios is almost endless.

On an individual level, experiences of grace are even more
diverse: John Wesley' experience of having his heart 'strangely
warmed' at a meeting in London's Aldersgate Street on 24 May
1738; St Paul's conversion on the road to Damascus;[70] Charles
Barff (1820-1860), a pioneer missionary in what later became
French Polynesia who grew into a living faith in God 'when at-
tending the flocks or herds of cattle in the fields my meditations
were sweet on the wonderful works of God';[71] Henry Vaughan
(1621/2-1695) who 'saw eternity the other night/ like a great
ring of pure and endless light'.[72] As Rabbi Lionel Blue has written:

> You come to God in many ways. A student I knew read the
> Summa of Thomas Aquinas, said 'that's it', threw up his ca-
> reer, changed his religion, and became a priest. Julian of

69. Psalms 95 and 122, for instance
70. Acts 9:1-19
71. quoted in Niel Gunson, *Messengers of Grace, evangelical missionaries in the South Seas 1797-1860*, OUP, 1978, page 52
72. Henry Vaughan, *The World*, lines 1-2

Norwich, in the Middle Ages, had a bad dose of 'flu, ran a temperature and saw visions.[73]

The list, again, is endless. The variety is breathtaking. Not all of it seems well-balanced. But yet, within the huge variety is the one constant: God. He is not always recognised, but 'He who knows God contemplates him in everything.'[74] He may not even always be there. But he most certainly does not stick just to the well-worn paths.

73. Rabbi Lionel Blue, *A Backdoor to Heaven*, DLT, 1979
74. Ibn 'Ata'Illah, *The Book of Wisdom (Kitab al-Hakim)* 17:163, trans Victor Danner, SPCK, 1979, page 88

CHAPTER 5

A Deep but Dazzling Darkness

He who denies God, denies himself. He who affirms God, affirms himself.[1]

(The Christian) finds he is in search of himself and comes to regard himself as an open question addressed to the future of God.[2]

God is not deduced from his gifts. He is known in his giving.[3]

Anyone who tries to describe the Ineffable Light in language is truly a liar – not because he hates the truth, but because of the inadequacy of his description.[4]

I am very aware, as I reach the climax of this book, that I am hovering incompetently on the brink of the indefinable. In this chapter I seek to bring together the threads of previous chapters to attempt an outline picture of God. Despite everything I have said – or, perhaps, because of it – I still think that this is an important, even if provisional, enterprise. Otherwise God is meaningless. The picture that I paint will, inevitably, be but partial – but will hopefully give the reader some idea of what my experience and my reason tell me of God. Doubtless this will at times seem to be an eclectic, not to say eccentric, mix of influences – but they are a mix of influences that ring true at a fundamental level, the level at which God alone is real.

Yet, they are not entirely random, because like most people my beliefs are moulded by my experience and my experience is in turn moulded by the Anglican Christian tradition in which I

---

1. Taittiriya Upanishad 2:6
2. Jürgen Moltman, *Theology of Hope*, SCM, 1967, page 91
3. David Jenkins, *The Contradiction of Christianity*, SCM, 1976, page 20
4. St Gregory of Nyssa (330-395) quoted in Kallistos Ware, *The Orthodox Way*, St Vladimir's Press, 1998, page 24

have been raised and in which I am ordained. That tradition is a mesh through which other experiences and other traditions are filtered. But, at the heart of anyone's picture of God is his or her own experience.

Marcus Aurelius, who was Roman Emperor in the second century AD, wrote 'so it is with the gods; it is experience which proves their power day by day, and therefore I am satisfied that they exist, and I do them reverence.'[5] As the great Muslim thinker of the Middle Ages, Al Ghazali, has argued, 'the highest type of knowledge ... is not that of reason or that of form, but that of direct experience. Thus the genuine knowledge of God belongs to this "experiential" order.'[6] Each of us picks and chooses what we find most congenial from both experience and the wider revelation, and what speaks to our own mind-set most vividly: that is the way we work, and we delude ourselves if we think otherwise. So the picture I draw today is not the picture I would have drawn as a young man in my 20s, nor is it be the same as I will draw when I am in my 70s. Yet there will be a continuum: a deepening of understanding, a fine-tuning of concepts, a rejection of some simplicities, a re-honing of old truths. Throughout all this, it is the one God to whom I will have been relating: his remarkable consistency lies most chiefly in the manner in which he relates to each of us, in the place where we are; because each one of us is different, and because we change as individuals, the unchanging God relates to us with an unchanging ability to be experienced in a way that speaks to our own deepest and most personal needs. And that will be different for each of us.

So, therefore, whatever I say in this chapter is both personal and universal; both time-specific and eternal. It is not, and can never be, definitive, but a picture of the God-I-know, expressed in words that mean something to me as I write. It is, I hope, a

5. Marcus Aurelius (121-180 AD), *Meditations 12:28*, trans M. Staniforth, Penguin, 1964 page 186
6. Majid Fakhry, *A History of Islamic Philosophy*, Longman, 1983, page 249

picture of God that grows out of a knowledge of God and not from illusion; it is a picture of God that, for me, sheds light on the perplexities of life; it is a picture of God that, despite all its limitations and potential absurdities is satisfying for me, here and now, at this point in my life. I offer it in the knowledge that it is incomplete, but in the hope that, even in its inadequacy, it may open a few doors for a few readers, and lead them on to a journey of wonder and of power.

As will be more than apparent by now, I am not easy with the certainties of revealed religion, narrowly interpreted, although my response to divine self-revelation is at the heart of everything I say. The Christian scriptures and, to a lesser extent, the scriptures of other faiths, inform everything I say – although as a starting point and not as straitjacket. Solid certainties have given way to the warp and weft of the interaction between revelation and experience, between tradition and reason. I am, in the words of Ziauddin Sardar, 'constantly on the boundaries of doubt'[7] – not because I doubt the divine reality, but because words and thoughts seem so inadequate when faced with that reality, and because he-who-I-am-seeking-to-conceptualise is so far beyond my ability to conceptualise.

I am certainly not content with any picture of God that portrays him as 'some grand architect of the universe who designed it, just like Basil Spence only bigger and less visible, … (as) … a top person in the universe who issues arbitrary decrees for the rest of the persons and enforces them because he is the most powerful being around.'[8] I am not content with God the policeman, God the Fireman, God the great big controlling microchip in the sky, or with any image that makes God static, like a forbidden idol of old. Descriptions of God such as this belittle him and make him smaller than our minds. These are childhood images, that need to be replaced in adulthood by a more rounded and nuanced – but still provisional – image. They need to be re-

7. Ziauddin Sardar, BBC Radio 3, 3 January 2005
8. Herbert McCabe, *God Matters*, Geoffrey Chapman, 1987, page 7

placed with a picture of God that is both mature and dynamic, both challenging and satisfying.

The God who is beyond knowledge
Theologians have long sought to prove the existence of God, an attempt that is now generally accepted as being futile. If his existence could be proved, in the same way as a mathematical theorem or the existence of water on Mars can be proved, he would be reduced to the same level. St Anselm of Canterbury (1033-1109) thought of God as, 'something than which nothing greater can be thought',[9] but ultimately that 'definition' is no more than a clever verbal devise to enable a logical proof of God to follow. Besides, as Karl Barth has pointed out, 'God has not the slightest need of our proofs.'[10]

'The name of our God is beyond comprehending: how can we understand?'[11] This, a question from within the Sikh tradition, is one that could be paralleled from all the great faiths. There is a sense amongst all believers that, when we approach God, we approach the limitless other. There is, furthermore, the sense that he is known not so much as an existential fact, but rather in the act of seeking:

He is beyond knowledge.
He is not this and not that.
He comes in the form those seek who truly turn to him
Yet that may not be his form.[12]

Thou mastering me
God! Giver of breath and bread;
World's strand, sway of the sea;
Lord of living and dead;

9. *Proslogion*, chap 2 in Benedicta Ward, *The Prayers and Meditations of St Anselm*, Penguin, 1973, page 244
10. Karl Barth, *Dogmatics in Outline*, SCM Press, 1949, page 38
11. W. H. McLeod, *Textual sources for the study of Sikhism*, Manchester University Press, 1984, page 49
12. Tiruvaymoli 2.5.9. Quoted in John Bowker, *God: a brief History*, Dorling Kindersley, 2002, page 98

Thou hast bound bones and veins in me, fastened me flesh,
And after it almost unmade, what with dread,
Thy doing: and dost Thou touch me afresh?
Over again I feel Thy finger and find Thee.[13]

To the religious mind, God is. Period. We know that fact, although how we know it is beyond our understanding. 'We know that he is, but not what he is'.[14] We take the leap of faith and then seek to move into deeper relationship with him. We come into contact with him who 'is above the known and above the unknown',[15] with him who transcends the limitations of symbol and language, while at the same time making sense of everything that is. We approach him who is anything we can express:

More affectionate than any friend,
More just than any ruler,
More loving than any father,
More a part of us than our own limbs,
More necessary to us than our own heart.[16]

We approach him for whom words are totally inadequate, he to whom silence is the most appropriate response: yet that very act, that very relationship, compels us to speak, to try and talk about him. The God who has had such an impact on us must be spoken about, in the same way as a lover must talk about the beloved. Yet this must be done with great caution, for those who 'would speak about God … (must) … speak with great humility and reverence. Do so as if you were in his presence.'[17] 'God is in heaven, and you upon earth: therefore let your worlds be few.'[18] It is in that spirit, I hope, that I write this chapter.

---

13. Gerald Manley Hopkins, *The Wreck of the Deutschland*
14. Maimonides, Guide 1.59, quoted in Bowker, op. cit. page 218
15. Kena Upanishad
16. St Nicholas Cabasilas (1322-) in Kallistos Ware, op. cit., page 12
17. August Hermann Franke, *Rules for the Protection of Conscience and for good order in conversation or in society*, 1689. Translation in *Piestists: selected writings*, ed Erb, SPCK, 1983, page 109
18. Ecclesiastes 5:2

The God who is worthy of worship

Throughout this book I have used superlatives when talking about God. It is almost as though we can only talk about him in two ways: either he is not this and not that (the classic *via negativa*), or he is the utmost example of any positive quality or attribute that we choose to name. Whenever we are bold enough to attempt to talk about him – I speak as a fool![19] – we run the risk of either anthropomorphism or anthropopathism (we give him human shape and human emotions). Although most people have moved beyond giving him human shape, we find it next to impossible not to infer to him human emotions. So long as we realise that, in so doing, we are only applying these concepts to him by analogy, as merest approximations of the depths and wonder of the reality, that is fine. God is he who is always more than we can ever think or say, and who is able to do far more abundantly than we can ever ask or think.[20] We need to talk about him, and analogy is all that we have to work with. 'All comparisons and likenesses fail to do justice to the Tree of Thy revelation and every way is a barrier to comprehension of the Manifestation of Thyself and the Dayspring of Thy Beauty.'[21]

This book has largely been about the limitations of language in talking about the ethereal other; the only appropriate responses seem to be analogy or silence. This God, the Wholly Other is bigger, better and more complete than even our most fervid imagination can ever comprehend. He is alone worthy of our worship and commitment. His is a Being that inspires, and occasionally elicits, a response of humbled awe. As Job put it when faced with God: 'I had heard of thee by the hearing of my ear, but now my eye sees thee; therefore I despise myself and repent in dust and ashes.'[22] The very name 'Islam' means 'submission'. The *Bhagavadgita* talks of 'surrendering all the desires of

19. 2 Corinthians 11:21
20. Ephesians 3:20
21. *Gleanings from the Writings of Bahá'u'lláh*, Baha'í Publishing Trust, 1976, page 4
22. Job 42:5-6

the heart' to God.[23] Religion generally – at least, theistic religion generally – is the act of submission and response towards God. Believing that God exists is not religion: acting on that belief in humble adoration is.

However, submission and adoration are not a one way street. God is not the slave-master, but One who wills to give of himself to those who seek. Therefore, any act of 'submission' is 'rewarded' by an amazing sense of liberation – the salvation, freedom and peace that we talked about in chapter 3. God is like a parent – the Father of Hosea[24] and the Abba of Jesus.[25] He is a prodigal father, a compulsive giver. Relating to God in faith is a life-long experience that seems somehow to 'ground' life in a sense of ultimate security and meaning, no matter how rough the surface may be. However great the problems of life there is a deep sense of God-given peace when and where it matters. When we are close to God we know that, despite everything, we are known and loved.

God the creator

Although we cannot prove the existence of God, we can infer his existence from his creation. 'There is not a thing but celebrates his praise.'[26] Fundamentally, God is the revealer who reveals himself. We have noted in chapter 4 how the believer can sense the self-communication of God in both work and word: in nature, in the cosmos, in art and literature, in human interaction. This involves an openness to 'the other', and a willingness to call that 'other' God. It is an act of faith that does this: for many secular folk will call that indefinable something by another name. God is there for those who want to see him, and who make the time to do so: that is perhaps why, in the stressed world of today, many just cannot understand the concept of God. Compare this with a very real sense of God – the three-mile-an-hour-God[27] –

23. *Bhagavadgita* 2:55
24. Hosea 11:1-4
25. Luke 11:2
26. Quran 17:44
27. Kosuke Koyama, *Three Mile an Hour God*, SCM, 1979

apparent in many slower, walking pace cultures where, according to one expert on African religion, 'there are no atheists'.[28] God is there, just as oxygen is there in the air, not always known by name, but ever-present and essential to life in any shape or form.

To many faiths, their starting point is that God is creator. The cycle of seasons, the power of natural forces only seem explicable when the hand of a creator God is discerned behind them. The Book Genesis and the gospel of John both start with passages that talk of creation and of God creating from nothing and perceiving it to be very good. Many of the names of God in the Old Testament are creation-related names: one possible meaning of the divine tetragrammaton YHWH is 'He who causes to be';[29] El Elyon, a title associated especially with Jerusalem, is 'He who made heaven and earth.'[30] God who creates by the power of his word is also the God who is known in Islam[31] and celebrated in the creeds of the Sikhs.[32] And throughout Africa 'creation is the most widely acknowledged work of God.'[33] God creates. It is in the creation that we can get some measure of the majesty of God. Creation is his primary calling card: 'Its words are but whispers; yet, if I understand them aright, it never ceases preaching.'[34] 'My book, philosopher, is the nature of created things, and whenever I wish I can read in the works of God.'[35]

The perception of creation being the good work of a good God is vital, for it gives life a positive meaning. If creation were merely neutral or even evil (as some Gnostics would have us believe) then life would be similarly cast and pointless. Yet we have to be realistic: there are plenty of times when it is hard to

28. John S. Mbiti, *African religions and Philosophy*, Heinemann, 1969, page 29
29. Exodus 3:14
30. Genesis 14:19
31. Quran 6:73
32. *Mul Mantra*, McLeod, op. cit., page 55
33. John S. Mbiti, op. cit., page 39
34. Cormac Ruadh Ó hUiginn, quoted in P. O'Dwyer, *Towards a History of Irish Spirituality*, Columba Press, 1995, page 145
35. Evagrius of Pontus quoted in Kallistos Ware, op. cit., page 43

affirm the goodness of creation and its creator, as when floods and earthquakes and tsunami strike. Even when we have factored out the destructive work of man in turning such natural events into natural disasters we are faced with a dilemma: creation is both delicate and beautiful, but also violent and horrendously powerful.

This is the dark side, so to speak. The God who, as we shall see, is both accessible and self-emptying, is also the God who the ancient Israelites associated with the volcanic phenomena of earthquakes, thunder, lightening, smoke and fire;[36] he is the God who none could look on and live.[37] He is a consuming fire[38] who can break out and destroy sinners.[39] God is the judge[40] who holds all humanity to strict account. He is the 'destroyer of all, as well as the creator of all',[41] a theme that is reiterated from Hinduism in which the Goddess Kali is seen as a destroyer, 'the terrifying aspect of divine creative energy'.[42]

This 'dark side' is as much part of God as those characteristics that we find easier to live with. They remind us that, despite everything, God is not just the mate-next-door (albeit a rather special one), but the creator of everything. In order to create something on the scale of this universe, you need stupendous ingenuity, imagination and raw power. God is not to be messed with: he who is Wholly Other needs to be treated with utmost respect.

So God is dangerous – but fascinating. We are drawn to him. It took the ancient Israelites many centuries to move from this primitive view of God (and primitive it is if left on its own) to a more mature and rounded one that began to recognise that there was more to God than brute force and intelligence. As their hist-

---

36. Exodus 19:16-18
37. Exodus 33:20
38. Deuteronomy 4:24; Hebrews 12:29
39. Leviticus 10:2; Numbers 16:35
40. Quran 7:8f; 21:47; 101:6-9
41. Dasam Granth, in W. L. McLeod, op. cit., page 56
42. *The Oxford Dictionary of World Religions*, ed Bowker, Oxford University Press, 1997, page 525

ory progressed and they began to recognise God at work in that history, they began to see that he was also a God of loving-kindness,[43] of justice to the poor and oppressed[44] and of love.[45] The knowledge that God is still the same God who appeared in so terrifying an aspect on Mount Sinai stops these later ideas from becoming too soft and mushy.

Yet this 'softer' aspect of God is also essential if he is not to degenerate into being an ogre. They are like flesh on a skeleton of steel. The Christian, and to some extent the Hindu, traditions are content to use the word love here.[46] Other cultures are more reticent with the concept: 'In their daily lives Africans do not talk much about love … (therefore) … we do not have many examples in which people talk about the love of God,'[47] and I cannot find the word used of God in the Quran. Yet, as in the Old Testament love is 'not the emotional or intellectual imposition of a favourable viewpoint, but his redeeming activity in human history'[48] so too we see Islam talking of God's compassion and mercy in the opening words of every sura (chapter) of the Quran. Muslims also, in their private prayer, think of God as a God of love: 'O God, make your love more precious to me than cool water to the thirsty.'[49] This is a divine love that wants the best for his creatures, yet will not coerce. It is outgoing and self-denying. This is the love of God, the gift of God, that strengthens its recipients, whatever faith they may adhere to, and whatever word they use to define the experience.

The Self-emptying God
God is often thought of as omniscient, omnipotent and omnipresent – all-knowing, all-powerful and present everywhere. I

---

43. Psalm 25:6-7
44. Psalm 82:3
45. Hosea 14:14
46. 1 John 4:16; Svetasvatara Upanishad 6
47. John S Mbiti, *Concepts of God in Africa*, SPCK, 1975, page 33
48. E. M. Good in the *Interpreter's Dictionary of the Bible*, Volume 3, Abingdon Press, 1962 page 166
49. Northern Ireland Inter-faith Forum calendar for February 2005.

am not comfortable with the first two of these, despite the fact
that they are a logical, even necessary, attribute of anything that
we would like to think of as divine. My problem with them is
that they are cold categories, evoking images of passionless
power – the great big microchip in the sky referred to above who
controls everything with robotic consistency. But, although
there is a very real way in which God, in order to be God, must
be omniscient and omnipotent, there is also a very real way in
which these attributes must be qualified.

In the Christian scheme of things, it is God himself who has
voluntarily qualified his own omnipotence and omniscience. He
has emptied himself, taken the form of a servant and become
obedient, even unto death.[50] Outside the Book of Revelation, the
New Testament never (except in Paul's second letter to the
Corinthians, and then only when quoting a passage from the
Old Testament[51]), calls God 'almighty', aware that, in Jesus,
power was made perfect in weakness. In Jesus, God is saying
that 'pure power', power as conventionally understood, is not
part of the nature of God. His is a power that is at ease with itself, secure in itself, a latent power that does not need to be expressed in the language of power. As Rowan Williams has put it,
paraphrasing St Gregory of Nyssa, we 'should wonder at the
power of God to make himself weak and identify himself with a
life not his own.'[52] His self-limitation in Christ 'becomes a sign
of his sovereign freedom from limitation, from the tyranny of
concepts.'[53] His is a power that is content to experience the un-
fairness of life even to the extent of becoming its victim.

This insight is not uniquely Christian, as each faith tradition
seeks to hold in balance the creative tension between power and
accessibility that is at the heart of God. Within Hinduism God

---

50. Philippians 2:6-8
51. 2 Corinthians 6:18
52. Rowan Williams, *The Wound of Knowledge*, Darton, Longman and
Todd, 1979, page 51
53. ibid, page 52

(in all his complexity) is seen 'not as a mere spectator, but a sharer in the travail of the world',[54] as the 'refuge and friend of all.'[55] God us very much he-who-comes-to-share with his creatures: 'Hindu mythology looks upon God as the eternal beggar waiting for the opening of the door that he may enter into the darkness and illuminate the whole horizon of our being as with a lightening flash. It is not so much man seeking God, as God seeking man. He goes out into the dangers of the wilderness to lead us out of it. God so loves the world that he gives himself to it.'[56] At the very centre of much Hindu piety is the picture of

The Lord taking birth as a human
Accepts this life with all its sorrow,
Coming here within our grasp
To raise us through suffering
To his Being as God.[57]

Here Hinduism, in a manner not unreminiscent of Christianity, tempers omnipotence with the many avatars (incarnations) of deity, and with a picture of God as 'mother of the Universe'.[58] This is a picture of God that resonates deeply with both my own experience, and with my Christian up-bringing. It is a description of the self-giving and solidarity of God.

Although within Islam Allah is the supreme ruler *par excellence*, 'wise and exalted in power'[59] there is the repeated refrain, at the opening of every sura of the Quran, that he is 'the compassionate, the merciful', the 'oft forgiving, most merciful.'[60] The popular belief, at least amongst Christians, that Muslims view Allah as utterly remote, and so totally without associate as to be distant and uncaring, is very far from the truth. He also is in solidarity with his creation. The great Muslim thinker of the so-called

54. Radhakrishnan, An Idealist View of Life, Unwin, 1908, page 265
55. Svetasvatara Upanishad 3:17
56. Radhakrishnan, op. cit., page 266
57. Tiruvaymoli 3.10.16 in John Bowker, God: a brief History, Dorling Kindersley, 2002, page 99
58. Bhagavadgita 9:17
59. Quran 31:9; 39:1
60. Quran 5:74

Middle Ages, Ibn Kaldun (1332-1402), went so far as to claim that the Islamic idea of the oneness of God with his creatures 'is identical with the incarnation the Christians claim for the Messiah. It is even stranger, in that it is the incarnation of something primeval in something created.'[61] God, as Ibn Khaldun saw him, was alongside his creatures, in a solidarity of being not dissimilar to that which Christians see manifested in Jesus, or the Hindus in the various avatars of their tradition. The Sikhs, while specifically rejecting any incarnation of God,[62] speak of him as 'my constant companion'[63] who 'suffers when the faithful grieve.'[64] So too the Jewish Rabbis, who saw God as suffering together with his children throughout their history.[65] It is a commonplace amongst those who are faced with tragedy, and still retain their faith, that God is alongside them. Despite the awesome destructive power of nature, or the cruelty of man, God is met as a helping hand, as a comfort in adversity, as a tempered omnipotence. There is an accessibility in God which makes it possible to love him: pure monad, remote and unfeeling, is neither attractive nor worthy of worship.

So too with omniscience. At the heart of much traditional piety, including my own, is there certainty that God knows what is going on within me, at the deepest level of my psyche. God is he who 'knows all that lies within, reading the deepest secrets of every human heart,'(Sikh)[66] and has 'two eyes that see well both by day and by night.'(Baronga people of Mozambique)[67] yet I do have problems transferring this to the macro level, to the political and cosmic field. Did God really know in advance that the Nazi's were going to murder six million Jews? Did he know that

---

61. Ibn Kaldun, *The Muqaddimah: an introduction to History*, trans F. Rosenthal, ed. N. J. Dawood, Routledge and Kegan Paul, 1967, page 363

62. *Mul Mantra* in McLeod, op. cit., page 55

63. Guru Arjan in McLeod, op. cit., page 50

64. *Benati Chaupi* in McLeod, op. cit., page 99

65. *The New Standard Jewish Encyclopaedia*, ed Roth and Wigoder, Massada Press, 1975, page 764

66. W. H. McLeod, op. cit., page 56. cf also Psalm 44:21

67. John S. Mbiti, *The Prayers of African religion*, SPCK, 1975, page 157

certain Hutu extremists were going to annihilate over a million of their Tutsi compatriots? And if he did, why didn't he stop it? Did he know that tsunami was to strike the Indian Ocean with such devastating effect in December 2004? It seems to me that God becomes callous if we think of him as omniscient: it makes more sense to see him as one who has placed us in a world of vast forces and vast beauty, and who has given us free will in that world. It is part of his voluntary abdication of power; it enables him to get involved with his creation, not just as an omniscient observer, but as a caring and supportive presence. God knows us intimately – I feel that in my bones – but I am not so sure that he knows the future. He has freely let that go.

God with us

So God is one to whom we can relate, not so 'other' that he is beyond our reach, yet not so like us that we can safely become over-familiar with him. He is at one and the same time the creator of the universe, and the One who comes alongside his creation in solidarity and grace. More – there is a very real sense in which he is not just a spiritual presence, but a spiritual immanence, present in the very fibre of his creation. He has put something of himself in the world he has created, and in the creatures he has created, not least humans who are made 'in the image of God'.[68] This is sometimes glimpsed in moments of special numinousity, as when Moses met with God in the burning bush.[69]

From earliest times humanity has sensed the presence of 'the other' in supposedly inanimate objects, and such sensitivity is common in the world of 'traditional religion'. The Ngombe people of the Congo think of God as 'the One who fills everything',[70] and many cultures pay elaborate respect to the spirits of particular places and objects, such as trees and streams. The Lugbara people of Uganda say 'We do not know what God is like: he is everywhere, in the wind and in the sky.'[71] William Blake once

68. Genesis 1:27
69. Exodus 3:2
70. John S. Mbiti, *Concepts of God in Africa*, SPCK, 1970, page 17
71. ibid, page 15

talked of seeing a tree 'full of angels'. Popular Islam, especially when it is geographically far from the centre, is full of mystical attachment to places that are meant to have a special sense of God: the village of Madarounfa in Niger is one such place to which pilgrims travel for miles in order to meet with God in the special atmosphere that surrounds its remarkable lake.

Our materialistic Western culture has largely lost this 'sixth sense'. Perhaps the Christian world has been suspicious of it because of its association with idolatry. Yet I believe that, despite inevitable vagueness, there is a real truth here: God is in some way intimate to and involved with his creation. The heavens tell of the glory of God.[72] I am not sure that I can go the whole way with pantheism, which states that everything is God, that likens our solar system to an atom of God and the planets as electrons orbiting the nuclear sun, but there does seem to be some mileage in the concept of a mutual inter-penetration between God and his creation. Christianity talks of Christ being in us[73] and of our being in Christ;[74] indeed, in one of his more poetic moments St Paul can even talk of Christ being in all things.[75]

Within Islam, with its strict prohibition of imagery and of anything that might even begin to smack of idolatry, such thoughts are harder to find. The Quran sees God as 'never absent',[76] 'closer to you than your jugular vein',[77] but that is almost certainly to be read as describing God as a spiritual presence rather than as an indwelling spirit. Within the Sufi tradition, however, such thoughts are almost commonplace: 'I looked into my own heart. In that, his place, I saw him.'[78]

This God within is also experienced in Hinduism: 'All this visible universe comes from my invisible Being. All beings have

---

72. Psalm 19:1
73. Ephesians 3:17; Colossians 1:27
74. 2 Corinthians 5:17
75. Colossians 1:17
76. Quran 7:7
77. Quran 50:16
78. Jalaludin Rumi (1207-1273), *He was in no other place*, in Idries Shah, *The Way of the Sufi*, Penguin, 1974, page 113

their rest in me.'[79] 'This is the spirit that is in my heart, greater than the earth, greater than the sky, greater than heaven itself, greater than all these worlds. This is the spirit that is in my heart.'[80] To the Sikhs he is equally 'immanent in sea, in earth, in sky.'[81]

There is more here than just heaven and earth singing creation's praise,[82] but rather a profound sense that creation and beauty are so beautiful and awe-inspiring that they are part of the divine self-revelation, a living example of the divine penetration of the created order, a divine penetration that gives context and reality both to that creation and to the divine. Creation is not God, but in some way speaks of God. Ibn 'Ata'Illah knew something of this when he wrote 'He who knows God contemplates him in everything.'[83]

I see something of God each hour of the twenty-four, and each moment then,
In the faces of men and women I see God, and in my own face in the glass.
I find letters from God dropt in the street, and every one is signed by God's name.[84]

Dismal days are awe-inspiring
Just watch a raindrop fall
And see within its fullness
The Upanishad of all.[85]

God is with us: that is a universal in all faiths. He is in us: that seems to me to be essential. But that he is also in some mysterious way in his creation also seems to me essential to a full and meaningful picture of God. Without it God moves into the mid-

79 *Bhagavadgita* 9:4
80. Chandogya Upanishad 3.13.7
81. W. McLeod, op. cit., page 56
82. Thomas Traherne, *The centuries of meditations I*, Psalm 19.1
83. Ibn 'Ata'Illah, *The Book of Wisdom* (Kitab al-Hikam) 17:163, trans Danner, SPCK, 1979, page 88
84. Walt Whitman (1819-1891), *Song of Myself*
85. Juvenile fragment by the author, c 1970

dle distance, both geographically and in terms of his relevance. And that is not the God I know.

God the First and the Last

I spoke above of 'the God I know'. That statement needs to be unpacked a bit, because my knowledge of God is very different from my knowledge of people or of science. There is a hidden-ness in God, an enigmatic inaccessibility: the God who reveals himself is also he who hides his face from his people.[86] He is both known and unknown, a 'deep but dazzling darkness',[87] a 'super-illuminated light of the great hidden-ness',[88] 'the fire-light of the great interiority',[89] 'the manifest and the hidden'.[90]

He is silence or a luminous void

He is effulgent life.

He is darkness within darkness.[91]

It is because God is 'unexplainable'[92] and beyond proof, it is be-cause he is beyond normal sense-experience, that people of all faiths have frequently lapsed into such paradox when talking about him. Paradox is a conjunction of opposites, working to-gether (in this instance) to explain what would otherwise be in-explicable: it is part of the grappling with truth that has so often been the theme of this book. The use of paradox, of creative ten-sion, allows us to put into tandem concepts that would, in the normal order of thing, not go together at all. By doing this, we underline the 'otherness' of what we are trying to describe, al-lowing for a sense of challenge and of mystery. This, I believe, is essential if our image of God is not to lapse into banality.

The Quran refers to God as 'The First and the Last, the

---

86. Deuteronomy 31:17; 32:20
87. Henry Vaughan (1621-1695), *The Night*
88. Jacob Boehme, *The Way to Christ*, trans Peter Erb, Paulist Press, 1978, page 96
89. ibid, page 89
90. Quran 28:88
91. Gopal Singh, *The Religion of the Sikhs*, Asia Publishing House, 1971 page 42
92. As the Ngombe of Congo, John S Mbiti, op. cit., page 15

Manifest and the Hidden',[93] a theme that is taken up in many other faith traditions. To Christians he is 'Alpha an Omega, the First and the Last, the Beginning and the End'.[94] To Hindus he is 'the Beginning and the Middle and the End of all things, their Seed of Eternity, their Treasure supreme.'[95] There is here an acknowledgement of the all-encompassing nature of God, creator of all that we know, guide for all that we live, and destiny of all that we are. There is, to lapse into technicality, an eschatological necessity in God, who gathers all things to himself when time and reincarnation are over. There is a sense here of God as the context of creation, from whom creation and eternity itself take their meaning: God, in fact, as ultimate truth.

The Personal God

The concept of truth, as we have seen in chapter 1, is a slippery thing – yet any concept of God worth entertaining views him as in some way the embodiment of truth. Pilate's question – what is truth?[96] – is changed into 'Who is Truth?' Truth becomes personal, and God (the personal God) is Truth in its fullest and most meaningful manifestation.

Yet even that concept – God as Truth personified – has its dangers. To think of God as personal in a sense reduces him to our level. As we have seen, there is a very real way, in all faith traditions, in which this movement has been of God's own volition and making, but nevertheless it does need to be treated with care lest he become a mere man. God is beyond personality – or at least beyond simple gender categorisation. I remember once, as a young curate, having an argument with a colleague as to the alternative merits of saying 'Our Father who art in heaven' and 'Our Father which art in heaven'. My colleague insisted that 'who' was far better in that it recognised God as a person. I was arguing that 'which', despite its impersonal connotations, better

---

93. Quran 28:88
94. Revelation 22:13
95. *Bhagavadgita* 9:18
96. John 18:38

preserved the mystery of God. God is person, yes, but he is not human. He is beyond personality. I am not sure who won the argument, but if I were to point out that my colleague is now a bishop …

There is a serious point here, which again hinges around the inadequacies of language. There is no word in most languages that can talk of God as both personal and as non-gender-specific. It is natural for most patriarchal societies to think of God as 'he': yet in the book Genesis God made both male and female in his/her own image.[97] We have no pronoun that can preserve the personality of God without being gender specific. If we say 'it', he/she becomes depersonalised. If we say he or she, he/she becomes falsely gender specific and we end up with gloriously tautological statements such as 'my mother, the Spirit'[98] or that wonderful statement from one of the 675 Council of Toledo that refers to Jesus being born 'from the womb of the Father'. The Finnish language has one such word – *Hän* – but since most of the world does not speak Finnish, it is of limited use outside Finland.

The Christian scriptures contain hints of God beyond gender: the Spirit of Genesis chapter one, who moves over the face of the waters, has been translated by some as doing so 'in a feminine manner'; and the figure of wisdom, there at creation in Proverbs chapter 8, is also feminine. There are rare instances of such an insight elsewhere, as in Julian of Norwich who 'saw that God was rejoicing to be our Father; rejoicing also to be our Mother.'[99]

Yes, God is personal, someone to whom we can relate in a personal way. He is not an 'it'. Yet he must not be constrained by any limiting concept of personality, but rather be allowed to transcend the rather porous boundaries we may have put around that concept. He is both personal and bigger than that.

---

97. Genesis 1:28
98. *The Gospel to the Hebrews* in E. Pagels, *The Gnostic Gospels*, Random House, 1979, page 6
99. Julian of Norwich (1342-1416), *Revelations of Divine Love*, chapter 52, trans Clifton Wolters, Penguin, 966, page 151

As the German-born American theologian Paul Tillich (1886-1965) has said, '"Personal God" does not mean that God is "a" person. It means that God is the ground of everything personal and that he carries within him the ontological power of personality. He is not a person, but he is not less than personal.'[100]

He is Truth, yet more than Truth. He is the beginning, Middle and End – yet beyond each and all of these. There is a beauty in God, a beauty in holiness, a 'beauty latent in his oneness'[101] – something ineffable and beyond either description or definition. Yet all these are abstracts and, although we cannot see him, God is most definitely not an abstract, or a concept, or a figment of the over-active imagination. We are struggling again to find adequate words to communicate something or someone that is way beyond words. How can you describe he-who-is-beyond-the-highest-thought yet is at the same time an ever-present and deeply personal reality?

God in sacrament
This is where the Christian concept of sacrament is so valuable, for it talks of God revealing himself in and through created matter in a way that is both personal and beyond personality. The classical Anglican definition of sacrament is 'an outward and visible sign of an inward and spiritual reality',[102] whereby something physical (the bread and the wine of the Communion, or the waters of Baptism) communicate something spiritual – indeed, *become* something spiritual, a means of grace and a harbinger of God. Teilhard de Chardin, in one of his wonderful meditations on the sacrament says: 'You came to me by means of a tiny scrap of created matter; and then, suddenly, you unfurled your immensity before my eyes and displayed yourself as

---

100. Paul Tillich, *Systematic Theology* I, University of Chicago Press, 1973
101. Sadruddin Qunawi, *An-Nafahat al-ilahiyyah* 60, quoted in the introduction *Fakhruddin 'Iraqi, Divine Flashes,* trans W. C. Chittick and P. L. Wilson, SPCK, 1982, page 25
102. From the Catechism, *Book of Common Prayer*, Columba Press, 2004, page 769

Universal Being.'[103] Teilhard's spirituality was centred very much on the bread and the wine of the Mass. Yet that bread and wine are a window on something much larger, a sense that in some way matter overflows and dissolves 'our narrow standards of measurement to reveal to us the dimensions of God'[104] in a sort of theological equivalent of Quantum Theory – or, rather, Quantum Experience.

My own feeling is that, to some extent, the traditional narrowing down of the concept of sacrament (two in Anglicanism, seven in Roman Catholicism), although understandable for historical reasons, is too narrow. The world is sacrament. Creation is sacrament. Humanity in the image of God is sacrament. The Church (the Body of Christ) is sacrament. Sacraments are all around us, ready to be picked up from the pavement. This is not very different from the verse in the *Bhagavadgita* that says 'When one sees Eternity in things that pass away and Infinity in finite things, then one has pure knowledge.'[105] It is a case of being open to the immaterial essence of things, and then allowing that immaterial essence to speak of the Other. We come back to the multifarious self-revelation of God that we looked at in the last chapter, to the God whose own internal dynamic compels him to communicate of himself to those open to receive.

The God who relates

It is not enough, however, just to say that he communicates 'of himself'. It is vital to know *what* he communicates. Here the scriptures and traditions of the various faith communities help ground what might otherwise be nothing more than a subjective response to the stimuli of life.

God is, first and foremost, a God who relates to the whole of his creation. He is life, and meaningful life is not something that can be experienced in isolation.

---

103. Teilhard de Chardin, *Le Milieu Divin: Meditation in time of War*, page 120
104. Teilhard de Chardin, *Hymn to Matter 8 August 1919*, in *Hymn of the Universe*, trans G. Vann, Fontana, 1973, page 64
105. *Bhagavadgita* 8:20

And God stepped out in space,
And he looked around and said:
I'm lonely –
I'll make me a world.[106]

Although I cannot go quite the whole way with Johnson and agree that God could be 'lonely', I do feel that there is some truth in the idea that God and his creation mutually complement and complete each other. It is part of God's voluntary abdication of power: by creating he admits himself to be needy of creation and in need of relationship in order to be fully God. He 'desires your presence and mine in the scheme of things unconditionally as parents delight in their children.'[107] The Christian experience has tried to package this in the concept of God as Trinity – a divine three-in-oneness that ensures that, integral to the unity of Godhead, there is a perfect and living relationship into which his followers are drawn.

'Trinity' sounds dreadfully abstract, and it is often portrayed as the driest of necessary dogmas. Yet the idea of Trinity is far from dry – although it is hard to avoid philosophical language when attempting to be precise as to exactly what is meant by it. The idea of Trinity took a while to be accepted by most Christian thinkers, not because it was felt to be wrong, but because it was felt to be difficult to square with that basic orthodoxy of the primary unity of God: 'Hear, O Israel, the Lord your God is One.'[108]

And they were right. There is something a-logical about Trinity. Not illogical, but a-logical, hard to square. But a statement nonetheless of fundamental truth. The so-called 'doctrine of the Trinity' was developed to explain how people of deep monotheistic faith could none the less experience Jesus and the Holy Spirit as fully God. The doctrine as classically formulated may be impossibly obtuse, but it is struggling with the inexplic-

106. James Weldon Johnson (1871-1938), *The Creation (A Negro Sermon from GOD'S TROMBONE, 1927)*. In *The Book of American Negro Poetry*, wd J. W. Johnson, Harcourt Brace and World, 1950, page 117
107. John V Taylor, *The Easter God*, Continuum, 2003, page 78f
108. Deuteronomy 6:4

able. God is one, yet he is experienced in many different ways, each different, each unique, each powerful – yet somehow all undeniably one.

This is part of the nature of God, a God who is relatively 'easy' to experience, yet who is also next to impossible to understand or explain. The concept of Trinity is the Christian attempt to make sense of the Christian experience of the God who reveals himself in a variety of ways, and whose primary purpose seems to be that of wishing to relate in love to both his creatures and his creation. Muslims have a not dissimilar experience of God, but have chosen to conceptualise that experience very differently. It is interesting that the Quran, on two occasions, refers to Jesus being 'strengthened by the Holy Spirit',[109] which would, from a Christian point of view at least, suggest that Islam, while strongly denying the divinity of Christ[110] or the possibility of Trinity,[111] is struggling to articulate a similar experience of God to that which Christians explain in terms of Trinity.

Part of the problem is that of translation. The doctrine of the Trinity was originally formulated in Greek and later in Latin, where the word used for 'person' is 'persona' – which means a mask. So what we are talking about is 'masks' or manifestations of God, recognisably the same actor, but playing different roles. These 'masks' are but different expressions of the One. It is all part of the same God, who is expressing himself in different ways according to circumstance. The same God who needs relationship comes to his people in many different ways,[112] each appropriate to culture and to context. A God who would do any less is hardly worthy of worldwide worship.

Talking of God

Christianity, in its attempt to 'make sense' of God has, at least in certain circles, done so in doctrinal and dogmatic terms. Another

109. Quran 2:87, 253
110. Quran 4:171; 5:17, 72
111. Quran 5:73
112. Hebrews 1:1-2

way of looking at God is to know him through his attributes. In Islam this has taken the form of the 99 beautiful names of God, each of which tells us something of who he is, and how he relates. They are names of essence and names of quality, names of mercy and names of majesty. He is The Great, The Opener, The Very Forgiving One, The Compassionate, The Inclusive, The Wise, He Who Forgives Freely, He Who Establishes Order, The Just, The Victorious ... There is, indeed, something for everyone in these names, just as there is something for everyone in God. What Islam has done here is very similar to what Christians have done when talking about Jesus, giving him multiple and exalted titles in an attempt to rise to the challenge of finding words to describe the impact he had on their lives: Saviour, Lord, Messiah, Son of God, Word of God ... Names, titles, are a noble attempt to come to grips with the mystery of God, to explain how he has impacted on the life of the faithful. They are an attempt to get a handle on the God-who-relates in words that mere mortals can understand. They begin to unpack the truth, but they never can be the whole truth.

Other traditions put greater emphasis on what God has done – although this is, of course, very far from absent in either Christianity or Islam. In the *Jap* of Guru Gobind Singh the faith Sikh notes that 'By Your deeds alone can You be known.'[113] The Jews have always told the story of what God has done for them, from taking them into his chosen people, leading them out of slavery in Egypt into the Promised Land and beyond. This story is told and retold at each Passover. This is the classic Jewish way. The Old Testament is commonly called 'Salvation History' – the history of the Israelites told from the point of view of faith. *'This is how God has been involved with us since the dawn of time.'* Theirs is a faith in an involved God, a faith that has frequently been tested to extremes, not least by the event of the Holocaust. Yet, despite obvious problems in believing in an 'involved God' in an unjust and disastrous world, few people of faith would choose to deny it outright. We feel that God is with us, alongside

113. McLeod, op. cit., page 93

us in solidarity. He is a God who makes himself real by relating to us, here and now. While we might no longer feel able to cling to the oversimplifications of believing that God is on our side, we can nonetheless continue to believe with integrity that the God of history is at our side. He is living and active, and he is here. If that were not so, God would be meaningless and irrelevant.

Why bother with God?

It is perhaps salient, as we come near the end of this book, to ask what the point of it all is. If what I have said contains any truth at all, how is it relevant today? What is the point of God? Don't folk manage very well without him?

It is all very well to agree that God exists, but what is the point of making a deliberate decision to allow him to impact on our lives – to move from theory to practice? It is a fair question, especially in a world where religion presents such a divided and often unattractive face. Being religious, accepting God as someone we want to do business with on a regular basis, doesn't always make people nicer. Therefore, the secular are entitled to ask, why bother?

It is extremely easy to point to all the negatives of religion – the crusades, inquisitions, indexes, jihads, suicide bombers, intolerance, self-righteousness etc. Yet that is not all there is to the story. Religion, admittedly, has all too often brought the worst out of people. But it has also frequently enhanced the best: monastic hospitality, the pioneers of prison and reform and the abolition of slavery, early hospitals and hospices, great art and great music. And that is before we get personal, and look at the simple goodness displayed day by day by so many people who take their impetus and their direction from their faith. I would argue that, very often, the negatives in religious practice are often the result of a false picture of God – the result of a narrow conception of God moulded in the image of our own worst human and culturally conditioned prejudices: but that is another book (at least).

The individual who takes the risk of responding to God's initiative takes a very real risk, and not just of being mocked at the dinner tables of polite society. There is a risk that it might be nonsense: but, then, that is faith. As Puddleglum puts it to the wicked witch queen in C. S. Lewis' *Silver Chair*: 'Suppose we have only dreamed, or made up those things .... Then all I can say is that, in that case, the made up things seem a good deal more important than the real ones. ... We're just babies making up a game, if you're right. But four babies playing a game can make a play world which licks your real world hollow. That's why I am going to stand by the play world.'[114] Or, as Kallistos Ware has put it in slightly more precise language: 'Faith in God enables me to make sense of things, to see them as a coherent whole, in a way that nothing else can do.'[115]

God brings an added dimension. When we allow him, he can link us to our deepest primal roots. When we are in a positive relationship with him, we are in touch with the power and the goodness and strength behind creation. That is a considerable asset – such an asset, indeed, that one could easily construct a self-interested argument for coming to faith. Yet, somehow, self-interest is low on anyone's list of reasons for conversion. More commonly there is a sense of gratitude towards God; believing in him is a response to a meeting with him – in scripture, in creation, in art, in music or in other people. Suddenly, because of God, life is filled with an electricity of purpose and meaning. Not-faith ceases to be an option. Belief in God brings contentment and peace.

This 'spiritual high' is unlikely to last, just as the first flush of courtship changes to the more mundane, but nonetheless real, love of domesticity. Something, someone, is there. In my pastoral ministry, I frequently hear people say that they 'are not alone'; an awareness of the presence of God cuts through the loneliness of their personal situation and makes it easier to bear. Similarly, I often hear folk say that they can't understand how

114. C. S. Lewis, *The Silver Chair*, Penguin, 1972, page 156
115. Kallistos Ware, op. cit., page 21

people cope without faith. Of course, many people do, after a fashion, and it is not always true that faith-folk cope any better. But, once we have met with the superabundant generousity of the living God, we can't run away. Life without him is life without a loved one:

> Take me to you, imprison me, for I
> Except you enthral me, never shall be free,
> Nor ever chaste, except you ravish me.[116]

Just as it is hard to talk of God without lapsing into cliché or unproductive paradox, so also it is hard to find the words to express the value of being in relationship with him. It is a liberating experience, as we saw from various faith traditions in chapter 3. It is also captivating, a 'slavery' that results in 'perfect freedom'.[117] It is something that demands the proverbial leap of faith whose worthwhile nature can never be proved by logic or argument. I cannot imagine life without that kernel of faith, yet am very fully aware of the inadequacy of my own response to the living God who exercises me so totally. May he grant me the grace to respond more adequately.

---

116. John Donne, *Holy Sonnet* from Poems of 1633
117. 2nd collect at Morning Prayer in the 1662 Prayer Book.